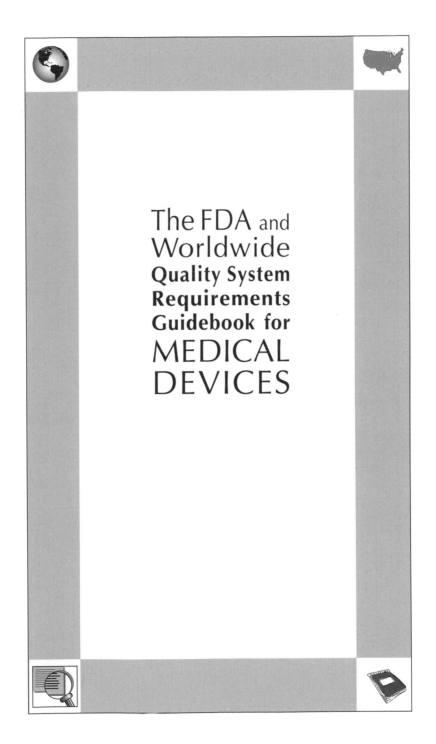

The FDA and Worldwide Quality System Requirements Guidebook for MEDICAL DEVICES

Also available from ASQ Quality Press

Eight-Step Process to Successful ISO 9000 Implementation:
A Quality Management System Approach
Lawrence A. Wilson

After the Quality Audit: Closing the Loop on the Audit Process
J. P. Russell and Terry Regel

The ISO 9000 Auditor's Companion
Kent A. Keeney

Managing Records for ISO 9000 Compliance
Eugenia K. Brumm

To request a complimentary catalog of publications,
call 800-248-1946.

The FDA and Worldwide Quality System Requirements Guidebook for MEDICAL DEVICES

Compiled by

Kimberly A. Trautman

GMP/Quality Systems Expert
Office of Compliance
Center for Devices and Radiological Health
U.S. Food and Drug Administration

ASQ Quality Press
Milwaukee, Wisconsin

*The FDA and Worldwide Quality System Requirements Guidebook
for Medical Devices*
Kimberly A. Trautman

Library of Congress Cataloging-in-Publication Data
Trautman, Kimberly A., 1964–
    The FDA and worldwide quality system requirements guidebook for
  medical devices/ Kimberly A. Trautman.
        p. cm.
    Includes index.
    ISBN 0-87389-377-8 (alk. paper)
    1. Medical instruments and apparatus industry—Law and
  legislation—United States. 2. Quality control—Law and
  legislation—United States. 3. Medical instruments and apparatus
  industry—United States—Quality control. 4. Medical instruments
  and apparatus industry—Law and legislation. 5. Quality control—
  industry—Quality control. I. Title.
    KF3827. M4T73 1997
    344.73'042—dc20
    [347.30442]   96-43156
                                                                      CIP

© 1997 by ASQ

10 9 8 7

ISBN 0-87389-377-8

Acquisitions Editor: Roger Holloway

ASQ Mission: To facilitate continuous improvement and increase customer
satisfaction by identifying, communicating, and promoting the use of quality
principles, concepts, and technologies; and thereby be recognized throughout
the world as the leading authority on, and champion for, quality.

Attention: Schools and Corporations
ASQ Quality Press books, audiotapes, videotapes, and software are available at
quantity discounts with bulk purchases for business, educational, or instruction-
al use. For information, please contact ASQ Quality Press at 800-248-1946, or
write to ASQ Quality Press, P.O. Box 3005, Milwaukee, WI 53201-3005.

For a free copy of the ASQ Quality Press Publications Catalog, including ASQ
membership information, call 800-248-1946.

Printed in the United States of America

♾ Printed on acid-free paper

American Society for Quality

Quality Press
611 East Wisconsin Avenue
Milwaukee, Wisconsin 53201-3005
800-248-1946
Web site http://www.asq.org

Contents

Introduction   1

Comparison Chart   5

SUBPART A General Provisions   15
  Scope   15
  Definitions   21

SUBPART B Quality System Requirements   27
  Quality Systems   27
  Management Responsibility   29
  Quality Audit   43
  Personnel   46

SUBPART C Design Controls   51
  Design Controls   51

SUBPART D Document Controls   77
  Document Controls   77

SUBPART E Purchasing Controls   87
  Purchasing Controls   87

SUBPART F Identification and Traceability   97
  Identification   97
  Traceability   98

SUBPART G Production and Process Controls   103
  Production and Process Controls   103
  Inspection, Measuring, and Test Equipment   116
  Process Validation   121

SUBPART H Acceptance Activities 125

Receiving, In-Process, and Finished Device Acceptance 125
Acceptance Status 136

SUBPART I Nonconforming Product 141

Nonconforming Product 141

SUBPART J Corrective and Preventive Action 149

Corrective and Preventive Action 149

SUBPART K Labeling and Packaging Control 159

Device Labeling 159
Device Packaging 161

SUBPART L Handling, Storage, Distribution, and
Installation 167

Handling 167
Storage 169
Distribution 171
Installation 175

SUBPART M Records 179

General Requirements 179
Device Master Record 182
Device History Record 184
Quality System Record 185
Complaint Files 186

SUBPART N Servicing 195

Servicing 195

SUBPART O Statistical Techniques 199

Statistical Techniques 199

Index 203

Introduction

HISTORY

Manufacturers establish and follow quality systems to help ensure that their products consistently meet applicable requirements and specifications. The quality systems for U.S. Food and Drug Administration (FDA)-regulated products (food, drugs, biologics, and devices) are known as current good manufacturing practices (CGMPs). Appropriate quality systems for medical devices are found in the quality system regulation. CGMP requirements for devices in part 820 (21 CFR part 820) were first authorized by section 520(f) of the Federal Food, Drug, and Cosmetic Act (the act) (21 U.S.C. 360j(f)), which was among the authorities added to the act by the Medical Device Amendments of 1976 (Pub. L. 94-295).

Under section 520(f) of the act, FDA issued a final rule in the July 21, 1978 *Federal Register* (43 FR 31508) prescribing CGMP requirements for the methods used in and the facilities and controls used for the manufacture, packing, storage, and installation of medical devices. This regulation became effective on December 18, 1978, and was codified under part 820.

The Safe Medical Devices Act of 1990 (the SMDA) (Pub. L. 101-629), enacted on November 28, 1990, amended section 520(f) of the act and provided FDA with the authority to add preproduction design controls to the CGMP requirements. This change in law was based on findings that a significant proportion of device recalls were attributed to faulty design of product. FDA found that approximately 44 percent of the quality problems that led to voluntary recall actions during a six-year period were attributed to errors or deficiencies that were designed into particular devices and may have been prevented by adequate design controls. These design-related defects involved both noncritical devices (for example, patient chair lifts, in vitro diagnostics, and administration sets) and critical devices (for example, pacemakers and ventilators).

The SMDA also added new section 803 to the act (21 U.S.C. 383), which, among other things, encourages FDA to work with foreign countries toward mutual recognition of CGMP requirements. FDA undertook the revision of the CGMP requirements to add the design controls authorized by the SMDA as well, because the agency believed that it would be beneficial to the public and the medical device industry for the requirements to be as consistent as possible with those contained in applicable international standards. These standards are, primarily, ANSI/ISO/ASQC Q9001-1994, *Quality Systems—Model for Quality Assurance in Design, Development, Production, Installation, and Servicing* (Milwaukee: ASQC), and the ISO draft international standard ISO/DIS 13485, *Quality Systems—Medical Devices—Particular Requirements for the Application of ISO 9001* (Geneva, Switzerland: International Organization for Standardization), dated April 1996.

In 1992 the Global Harmonization Task Force (GHTF) was formed in an effort to harmonize regulatory requirements for the medical device industry. The GHTF includes representatives of the Canadian Ministry of Health and Welfare; the Japanese Ministry of Health and Welfare; FDA; industry members from the European Union, Australia, Canada, Japan, and the United States; and a few delegates from observing countries. Currently, the GHTF has four study groups: Study Group 1 works on harmonizing device approval aspects; Study Group 2 works on harmonizing requirements, forms, and guidances on postmarket surveillance and vigilance reporting; Study Group 3 works on harmonizing quality system requirements, as well as drafting harmonized guidance documents on quality system subjects; and Study Group 4 works on harmonizing aspects around the regulatory auditing of quality systems.

Regulatory requirements for medical devices are being developed and revised by many different countries and trading blocks now and have been for the past few years. The GHTF has played an important role in trying to harmonize those requirements. To date, the most successful effort has been the harmonization of the quality system requirements. There appears to be consensus that quality system requirements should incorporate the principles of ISO 9001 plus additional requirements specific to the medical device sector. ISO Technical Committee 210, Quality Management and Corresponding General Aspects for Medical Devices, is attempting, through the ISO/DIS 13485 standard, to capture the harmonized additional requirements that are particular to medical devices.

FDA supports the international harmonization of standards and regulations governing medical devices and the eventual mutual recognition of CGMP inspections between major device markets. While full achievement of this goal is still in the future, the harmonization of quality standards is an important first step. FDA believes in a stepwise approach toward harmonization and eventual mutual recognition. For CGMP inspections or Quality System Conformity Assessments, these goals comprise four basic steps.

First, the harmonization of quality system requirements is a building block of all future work in this area. FDA believes that by working with the GHTF, specifically Study Group 3, it has developed a quality system regulation that incorporates the harmonized quality system requirements that are recognized around the world. The second step is the harmonization of regulatory auditing or compliance inspections. This work is currently underway in the GHTF in Study Group 4, which has developed a draft document entitled "Guidelines for Regulatory Auditing Quality Systems of Medical Device Manufacturers," expected to be finalized in 1997.

The third step is for harmonization of the policy, interpretation, and regulatory consequences of noncompliance with the quality system requirements in the United States and in counterpart requirements of other countries. The fourth step is the actual negotiation of the mutual recognition agreement between the two applicable parties. Underlying these activities is an ongoing need for confidence building between the parties working toward mutual recognition.

FDA believes that the quality system regulation will provide a sound foundation for the goal of mutual recognition of inspections, a goal that will benefit industry as well as FDA.

THIS GUIDEBOOK

The principle objective of this guidebook is to provide individuals with a concise guide for understanding and implementing quality system requirements for medical devices in the United States and worldwide. This book is a compilation of several documents. Each section breaks into three major areas for each subpart of the FDA's quality system regulation. Each subpart of the regulation has requirement sections, guidance sections, and a section for the reader's notes.

The requirements sections contain the following:

The FDA regulatory requirements as found in the final quality system regulation (21 CFR § 820) published in the *Federal Register* in October 1996 are given. Where applicable, the corresponding section(s) from the FDA's 1978 Good Manufacturing Practice (GMP) regulation are referenced. These two sections comprise the U.S. quality system requirements for medical devices, present and past.

ASQC/ISO/ANSI 9001-1994, *Quality Systems—Model for Quality Assurance in Design, Development, Production, Installation, and Servicing* requirements are listed. Where applicable, the corresponding section(s) from the ISO/DIS 13485:April 1996, *Quality Systems—Medical Devices—Particular Requirements for the Application of ISO 9001* (available from the Association for the Advancement of Medical Instrumentation, 3330 Washington Boulevard, Suite 400, Arlington, VA 22201-4598, telephone number 703-525-4890), are referenced. These two sections constitute the worldwide quality system requirements for medical devices.

The guidance sections are made up of two elements. First, corresponding to the requirements being discussed, is FDA guidance. This guidance consists of excerpts from the preamble to the final quality system regulation published in the *Federal Register* in September 1996. Second is guidance prepared by the GHTF. The GHTF guidance document is entitled *Guidance on Quality Systems for the Design and Manufacture of Medical Devices*, issue 7, dated August 1994. The GHTF's guidance document was broken down into requirement sections and organized according to the corresponding requirements from FDA's quality system regulation.

This guidebook also contains, in the chart on pages 5–14, a side-by-side comparison of the FDA's 1996 quality system regulation versus the FDA's 1978 GMP regulation versus the ISO 9001:1994 and 1996 ISO/DIS 13485 requirements.

While this guidebook is meant to be a long-standing reference book, it is also meant to be utilized in conjunction with the four-hour series of videotapes entitled *New Quality System Regulation*, produced by FDA's Center for Devices and Radiological Health Media Studio. The videotape series and this guidebook are a part of the phase I training program on the FDA's quality system regulation. Copies of the videotapes may be purchased through National Technical Information Services (NTIS), 5285 Port Royal Road, Springfield, VA 22161, telephone number 800-553-6847. Copies of the videotapes may also be available through medical device associations and societies.

COMPARISON CHART

1996 QUALITY SYSTEM REGULATION
VERSUS
1978 GOOD MANUFACTURING PRACTICES REGULATION
VERSUS
ANSI/ISO/ASQC Q9001-1994 AND ISO/DIS 13485:1996

Quality System Regulation 1996: 21 CFR § 820	Good Manufacturing Practices (GMP) Regulation 1978: 21 CFR § 820	ANSI/ISO/ASQC Q9001-1994 and ISO/DIS 13485:April 1996	
§ 820.1 Scope	§ 820.1 Scope	9001	1 Scope
		13485	1 Scope
		9001	2 Normative references
		13485	2 Normative References
§ 820.3 Definitions	§ 820.3 Definitions	9001	3 Definitions
		13485	3 Definitions
§ 820.5 Quality system	§ 820.5 Quality assurance program	9001	4 Quality system requirements
		9001	4.2 Quality system
		9001	4.2.1 General
		13485	4.2.1 General
§ 820.20 Management responsibility		9001	4.1 Management responsibility
§ 820.20(a) Quality policy		9001	4.1.1 Quality policy

Quality System Regulation 1996: 21 CFR § 820	Good Manufacturing Practices (GMP) Regulation 1978: 21 CFR § 820	ANSI/ISO/ASQC Q9001-1994 and ISO/DIS 13485:April 1996
§ 820.20(b) Organization	§ 820.20 Organization	9001 4.1.2 Organization
§ 820.20(b)(1) Responsibility and authority	§ 820.20 Organization	9001 4.1.2.1 Responsibility and authority
§ 820.20(b)(2) Resources	§ 820.20 Organization	9001 4.1.2.2 Resources
§ 820.20(b)(3) Management representative	§ 820.20 Organization § 820.20(a)(4) Quality assurance program requirements	9001 4.1.2.3 Management representative 9001 4.2.2(b) Quality-system procedures
§ 820.20(c) Management review		9001 4.1.3 Management review
§ 820.20(d) Quality planning		9001 4.2.3 Quality planning
§ 820.20(e) Quality system procedures		9001 4.2.2 Quality-system procedures 9001 4.2.1 General
§ 820.22 Quality audit	§ 820.20(b) Audit procedures	9001 4.17 Internal quality audits
§ 820.25 Personnel		9001 4.18 Training
§ 820.25(a) General	§ 820.25 Personnel	9001 4.1.2.2 Resources
§ 820.25(b) Training	§ 820.25(a) Personnel training	9001 4.18 Training

Quality System Regulation 1996: 21 CFR § 820	Good Manufacturing Practices (GMP) Regulation 1978: 21 CFR § 820	ANSI/ISO/ASQC Q9001-1994 and ISO/DIS 13485:April 1996
§ 820.30 Design controls		9001 4.4 Design Control
§ 820.30(a) General		9001 4.4.1 General
§ 820.30(b) Design and development planning		9001 4.4.2 Design and development planning 9001 4.4.3 Organizational and technical interfaces
§ 820.30(c) Design input		9001 4.4.4 Design input
§ 820.30(d) Design output		9001 4.4.5 Design output
§ 820.30(e) Design review		9001 4.4.6 Design review
§ 820.30(f) Design verification		9001 4.4.7 Design verification
§ 820.30(g) Design validation	§ 820.160 Finished device inspection (simulated use testing)	9001 4.4.8 Design validation 13485 4.4.1 General *13485 4.4.8 Design validation*
§ 820.30(h) Design transfer	§ 820.100 Manufacturing specifications and processes § 820.100(a)(1) Specification controls	9001 4.2.3(c) Quality planning 9001 4.4.1 General

Quality System Regulation 1996: 21 CFR § 820	Good Manufacturing Practices (GMP) Regulation 1978: 21 CFR § 820	ANSI/ISO/ASQC Q9001-1994 and ISO/DIS 13485:April 1996
§ 820.30(i) Design changes	§ 820.100(a)(2) Specification controls	9001 4.4.9 Design changes
§ 820.30(j) Design history file		9001 4.16 Control of quality records
§ 820.40 Document controls		9001 4.5 Document and data control 9001 4.5.1 General
§ 820.40(a) Document approval and distribution	§ 820.180 General requirements	9001 4.5.2 Document and data approval and issue *13485 4.5.2 Document and data approval and issue*
§ 820.40(b) Document changes	§ 820.180 General requirements	9001 4.5.3 Document and data changes
§ 820.50 Purchasing controls		9001 4.6 Purchasing 9001 4.6.1 General
§ 820.50(a) Evaluation of suppliers, contractors, and consultants	§ 820.81(a) Acceptance of critical components	9001 4.6.2 Evaluation of subcontractors
§ 820.50(b) Purchasing data	§ 820.80(b) Critical component supplier agreement	9001 4.3 Contract review 9001 4.6.3 Purchasing data *13485 4.6.3 Purchasing data*

Quality System Regulation 1996: 21 CFR § 820	Good Manufacturing Practices (GMP) Regulation 1978: 21 CFR § 820	ANSI/ISO/ASQC Q9001-1994 and ISO/DIS 13485:April 1996
§ 820.60 Identification	§ 820.80 Components	9001 4.8 Product identification and traceability *13485 4.8(A) Product identification and traceability*
§ 820.65 Traceability	§ 820.151 Critical device, distribution records	9001 4.8 Product identification and traceability *13485 4.8(B) Product identification and traceability*
§ 820.70 Production and process controls		9001 4.9 Process control
§ 820.70(a) General	§ 820.100 Manufacturing specifications and processes § 820.100(b)(1) and (2) Processing controls	9001 4.9 (a)(c)(d)(e) and (f) Process control
§ 820.70(b) Production and process changes	§ 820.100(b)(3) Processing controls	9001 4.4.9 Design changes
§ 820.70(c) Environmental control	§ 820.46 Environmental control	9001 4.9(b) Process control 9001 4.11.2(g) Control procedure *13485 4.9(B) Environmental control in manufacture*

Quality System Regulation 1996: 21 CFR § 820	Good Manufacturing Practices (GMP) Regulation 1978: 21 CFR § 820	ANSI/ISO/ASQC Q9001-1994 and ISO/DIS 13485:April 1996
§ 820.70(d) Personnel	§ 820.25(b) Personnel health and cleanliness § 820.56(a) Personnel sanitation § 820.56(c) Personnel practices	9001 4.9(b) Process control *13485 4.9(A) Personnel*
§ 820.70(e) Contamination control	§ 820.56(b) Contamination control § 820.56(d) Sewage and refuse disposal	9001 4.9(b) Process control *13485 4.9(C) Cleanliness of product*
§ 820.70(f) Buildings	§ 820.40 Buildings	9001 4.9(b) Process control
§ 820.70(g) Equipment	§ 820.60(a)(b) and (c) Equipment	9001 4.9(b) and (g) Process control *13485 4.9(D) Maintenance*
§ 820.70(h) Manufacturing material	§ 820.60(d) Manufacturing material	9001 4.9(b) Process control
§ 820.70(i) Automated processes	§ 820.61 Measurement equipment § 820.195 Critical devices, automated data processing	9001 4.4.8 Design validation *13485 4.9(F) Computer software used in process control*
§ 820.72 Inspection, measuring, and test equipment	§ 820.61 Measurement equipment	9001 4.11 Control of inspection, measuring, and test equipment

10

Quality System Regulation 1996: 21 CFR § 820	Good Manufacturing Practices (GMP) Regulation 1978: 21 CFR § 820	ANSI/ISO/ASQC Q9001-1994 and ISO/DIS 13485:April 1996
§ 820.75 Process validation	§ 820.100(a)(1) Specification controls § 820.101 Critical devices, manufacturing specifications, and processes	9001 4.9 Process control *13485 4.9 Process control*
§ 820.80 Receiving, in-process, and finished device acceptance		9001 4.10 Inspection and testing
§ 820.80(a) General	§ 820.80 Components	9001 4.10.1 General 9001 4.6.4 Verification of purchased product 9001 4.7 Control of customer-supplied product
§ 820.80(b) Receiving acceptance activities	§ 820.80(a) Acceptance of components	9001 4.10.2 Receiving inspection and testing
§ 820.80(c) In-process acceptance activities		9001 4.10.3 In-process inspection and testing
§ 820.80(d) Final acceptance activities	§ 820.160 Finished device inspection	9001 4.10.4 Final inspection and testing
§ 820.80(e) Acceptance records	§ 820.20(a)(2) Quality assurance program requirements § 820.161 Critical devices, finished device inspection	9001 4.10.5 Inspection and test records *13485 4.10.5 Inspection and test records*

Quality System Regulation 1996: 21 CFR § 820	Good Manufacturing Practices (GMP) Regulation 1978: 21 CFR § 820	ANSI/ISO/ASQC Q9001-1994 and ISO/DIS 13485:April 1996
§ 820.86 Acceptance status	§ 820.80(b) Storage and handling of components § 820.160 Finished device inspection	9001 Inspection and test status
§ 820.90 Nonconforming product		9001 4.13 Control of Nonconforming Product
§ 820.90(a) Control of nonconforming product	§ 820.161 Critical devices, finished device inspection	9001 4.13.1 General
§ 820.90(b) Nonconforming review and disposition	§ 820.115 Reprocessing of devices or components § 820.116 Critical devices, reprocessing of devices or components	9001 4.13.2 Review and disposition of nonconforming product 13485 4.13.2 Review and disposition of nonconforming product
§ 820.100 Corrective and preventive action	§ 820.20(a)(3) Quality assurance program requirements § 820.162 Failure investigation	9001 4.14 Corrective and preventive action 13485 4.14 Corrective and preventive action
§ 820.120 Device labeling	§ 820.120 Device labeling § 820.121 Critical devices, device labeling	9001 4.15.1 General 9001 4.15.4 Packaging 13485 4.15.4 Packaging
§ 820.130 Device packaging	§ 820.130 Device packaging	9001 4.15.1 General 9001 4.15.4 Packaging

Quality System Regulation 1996: 21 CFR § 820	Good Manufacturing Practices (GMP) Regulation 1978: 21 CFR § 820	ANSI/ISO/ASQC Q9001-1994 and ISO/DIS 13485:April 1996
§ 820.140 Handling	§ 820.80(b) Storage and handling of components	9001 4.15.1 General 9001 4.15.2 Handling *13485 4.15.1 General*
§ 820.150 Storage	§ 820.80(b) Storage and handling of components	9001 4.15.1 General 9001 4.15.3 Storage 9001 4.15.5 Preservation *13485 4.15.1 General*
§ 820.160 Distribution	§ 820.150 Distribution § 820.151 Critical devices, distribution records	9001 4.15.1 General 9001 4.15.6 Delivery 9001 4.3 Contract review *13485 4.15.6 Delivery* *13485 4.8(B) Traceability*
§ 820.170 Installation	§ 820.152 Installation	9001 4.9 Process control *13485 4.9(E) Installation*
§ 820.180 General requirements	§ 820.180 General requirements	9001 4.16 Control of quality records 9001 4.5 Document and data control 9001 4.5.1 General *13485 4.16 Control of quality records*

Quality System Regulation 1996: 21 CFR § 820	Good Manufacturing Practices (GMP) Regulation 1978: 21 CFR § 820	ANSI/ISO/ASQC Q9001-1994 and ISO/DIS 13485:April 1996
§ 820.181 Device master record	§ 820.181 Device master record § 820.182 Critical devices, device master record	9001 4.16 Control of quality records 9001 4.2.2 Quality-system procedures 13485 4.2.3 Quality planning
§ 820.184 Device history record	§ 820.184 Device history record § 820.185 Critical devices, device history record § 820.20(a)(1) Quality assurance program requirements	9001 4.16 Control of quality records 13485 4.16 Control of quality records
§ 820.186 Quality system record		9001 4.16 Control of quality records 9001 4.2.2 Quality-system procedures
§ 820.198 Complaint files	§ 820.198 Complaint files	9001 4.14.1 General 9001 4.14.2 Corrective action 9001 4.14.3 Preventive action 13485 4.14.1 General
§ 820.200 Servicing	§ 820.20(a)(3) Quality assurance program requirements	9001 4.19 Servicing
§ 820.250 Statistical techniques	§ 820.81(a) Acceptance of critical components § 820.160 Finished device inspection	9001 4.20 Statistical techniques

General Provisions

 FDA QUALITY SYSTEM REGULATION—1996

§ 820.1 Scope

§ 820.1(a) *Applicability.* (1) Current good manufacturing practice (CGMP) requirements are set forth in this quality system regulation. The requirements in this part govern the methods used in, and the facilities and controls used for, the design, manufacture, packaging, labeling, storage, installation, and servicing of all finished devices intended for human use. The requirements in this part are intended to ensure that finished devices will be safe and effective and otherwise in compliance with the Federal Food, Drug, and Cosmetic Act (the act). This part establishes basic requirements applicable to manufacturers of finished medical devices. If a manufacturer engages in only some operations subject to the requirements in this part, and not in others, that manufacturer need only comply with those requirements applicable to the operations in which it is engaged. With respect to class I devices, design controls apply only to those devices listed in § 820.30(a)(2). This regulation does not apply to manufacturers of components or parts of finished devices, but such manufacturers are encouraged to use appropriate provisions of this regulation as guidance. Manufacturers of human blood and blood components are not subject to this part, but are subject to part 606 of this chapter.

(2) The provisions of this part shall be applicable to any finished device as defined in this part, intended for human use, that is manufactured, imported, or offered for import in any State or Territory of the United States, the District of Columbia, or the Commonwealth of Puerto Rico.

(3) In this regulation the term "where appropriate" is used several times. When a requirement is qualified by "where appropriate," it is deemed to be "appropriate" unless the manufacturer can document justification otherwise. A requirement is "appropriate" if nonimplementation could reasonably be expected to result in the product not meeting its specified requirements or the manufacturer not being able to carry out any necessary corrective action.

§ 820.1(b) *Limitations.* The quality system regulation in this part supplements regulations in other parts of this chapter except where explicitly stated otherwise. In the event that it is impossible to comply with all applicable regulations, both in this part and in other parts of this chapter, the regulations specifically applicable to the device in question shall supersede any other generally applicable requirements.

§ 820.1(c) *Authority.* Part 820 is established and issued under authority of sections 501, 502, 510, 513, 514, 515, 518, 519, 520, 522, 701, 704, 801, 803 of the Federal Food, Drug, and Cosmetic Act (the act) (21 U.S.C. 351, 352, 360, 360c, 360d, 360e, 360h, 360i, 360j, 360l, 371, 374, 381, 383). The failure to comply with any applicable provision in this part renders a device adulterated under section 501(h) of the act. Such a device, as well as any person responsible for the failure to comply, is subject to regulatory action.

§ 820.1(d) *Foreign manufacturers.* If a manufacturer who offers devices for import into the United States refuses to permit or allow the completion of a Food and Drug Administration (FDA) inspection of the foreign facility for the purpose of determining compliance with this part, it shall appear for purposes of section 801(a) of the act, that the methods used in, and the facilities and controls used for, the design, manufacture, packaging, labeling, storage, installation, or servicing of any devices produced at such facility that are offered for import into the United States do not conform to the requirements of section 520(f) of the act and this part and that the devices manufactured at that facility are adulterated under section 501(h) of the act.

§ 820.1(e) *Exemptions or variances.* (1) Any person who wishes to petition for an exemption or variance from any device quality system requirement is subject to the requirements of section 520(f)(2) of the act. Petitions for an exemption or variance shall be submitted according to the procedures set forth in § 10.30 of this chapter, the FDA's administrative procedures. Guidance is available from the Center for Devices and Radiological Health, Division of Small Manufacturers Assistance, (HFZ-220), 1350 Piccard Dr., Rockville, MD 20850, U.S.A., telephone 800-638-2041 or 301-443-6597, FAX 301-443-8818.

(2) FDA may initiate and grant a variance from any device quality system requirement when the agency determines that such variance is in the best interest of the public health. Such variance will remain in effect only so long as there remains a public health need for the device and the device would not likely be made sufficiently available without the variance.

1978: § 820.1 SCOPE

 ANSI/ISO/ASQC Q9001-1994

1 Scope

This American National Standard specifies quality-system requirements for use where a supplier's capability to design and supply conforming product needs to be demonstrated.

The requirements specified are aimed primarily at achieving customer satisfaction by preventing nonconformity at all stages from design through to servicing.

This American National Standard is applicable in situations when

a) design is required and the product requirements are stated principally in performance terms, or they need to be established, and

b) confidence in product conformance can be attained by adequate demonstration of a supplier's capabilities in design, development, production, installation, and servicing.

NOTE 1 For informative references, see annex A.

2 Normative references

The following standard contains provisions which, through reference in this text, constitute provisions of this American National Standard. At the time of publication, the edition indicated was valid. All standards are subject to revision, and parties to agreements based on this American National Standard are encouraged to investigate the possibility of applying the most recent edition of the standard indicated below. The American National Standards Institute and members of IEC and ISO maintain registers of currently valid American National Standards and International Standards.

ISO 8402:1994, *Quality management and quality assurance—Vocabulary.*

ALSO SEE ISO/DIS 13485:1996,1 SCOPE AND 2 NORMATIVE REFERENCES

 **FDA GUIDANCE**

§ 820.1 Scope

The principles embodied in this quality system regulation have been accepted worldwide as a means of ensuring that acceptable products are produced. The regulation has been harmonized with the medical device requirements in Europe, Australia, and Japan, as well as the requirements proposed by Canada, and it is anticipated that other countries will adopt similar requirements in the near future.

FDA, however, did not adopt ISO 9001:1994 verbatim for two reasons. First, there were complications in dealing with the issue of copyrights, and, second, FDA does not believe that ISO 9001:1994 alone is sufficient to adequately protect the public health. Therefore, FDA has worked closely with the GHTF and ISO Technical Committee (TC) 210 to develop a regulation that is consistent with both ISO 9001:1994 and ISO/CD 13485. FDA made several suggestions to TC 210 on the drafts of the ISO/CD 13485 document in order to minimize differences and move closer to harmonization. In some cases, FDA has explicitly stated requirements that many experts believe are inherent in ISO 9001:1994. Through the many years of experience enforcing and evaluating compliance with the original CGMP regulation, FDA has found that it is necessary to clearly spell out its expectations. This difference in approach does not represent any fundamentally different requirements that would hinder global harmonization. In fact, numerous comments expressed approval and satisfaction with FDA's effort to harmonize the quality system requirements with those of ISO 9001:1994 and ISO/CD 13485.

This regulation provides the "basic" requirements for the design and manufacture of medical devices. The requirements are written in general terms to allow manufacturers to establish procedures appropriate for their devices and operations. Also, as just discussed, a manufacturer need only comply with those requirements applicable to the operations in which he or she is engaged. Because the regulation requirements are basic, however, they will apply in total to most manufacturers subject to the regulation. The extent of the documentation necessary to meet the regulation requirements may vary with the complexity of the design and manufacturing operations, the size of the firm, the importance of a process, and the risk associated with the failure of the device, among other factors. Small manufacturers may design acceptable quality systems that require a minimum of documentation and, where possible, may automate documentation. In many situations, documentation may be kept at a minimum by combining many of the record-keeping requirements of the regulation, for example, the production standard operating procedures (SOPs), handling, and storage procedures. When manufacturers believe that the requirements are not necessary for their operations, they may petition for an exemption or variance from all or part of the regulation pursuant to section 520(f)(2) of the act.

FDA added § 820.1(a)(3) on how to interpret the phrase "where appropriate" in the regulation, as recommended by the GMP Advisory Committee. This section is consistent with the statement in ISO/CD 13485.

 **GHTF GUIDANCE**

1 Scope

This document provides general guidance on the implementation of quality systems for medical devices based on ISO 9001. Such quality systems include those of the EU Medical Device Directives and the GMP requirements currently in preparation in Canada, Japan, and the USA. The guidance given in this document is applicable to the design, development, production, installation, and servicing of medical devices of all kinds.

This document describes concepts and methods to be considered by medical device manufacturers who are establishing and maintaining quality systems. It is not intended to be directly used for assessment of quality systems. This document describes examples of ways in which the quality system requirements can be met, recognizing that there may be alternative ways that are better suited to a particular device/manufacturer.

2 References

ISO/DIS 9001.2:1994, *Quality systems—Model for quality assurance in design/development, production, installation and servicing.*

ISO 9004-1:1994, *Quality management and quality system elements—Part 1: Guidelines.*

ISO 8402:1993, *Quality—Vocabulary.*

EN 46001:1993, *Quality Systems—Medical Devices—Particular Requirements for the Application of EN 29001.*

ISO 9000-2:1993, *Generic guidelines for the application of ISO 9001, ISO 9002 and ISO 9003.*

EN 724:1993, *Guidance on the application of EN 29001/EN 46001 and EN 29002/EN 46002 for non-active medical devices.*

prEN 928:1991, *Guidance on the application of EN 29001/EN 46001 and EN 29002/EN 46002 for the in-vitro diagnostics industry.*

prEN 61272:1993, *Guidance on the application of ISO 9001/EN 46001 and ISO 9002/EN 46002 for the active medical device industry.*

§ 820.3 Definitions

(a) **Act** means the Federal Food, Drug, and Cosmetic Act, as amended (secs. 201-903, 52 Stat. 1040 *et seq.*, as amended (21 U.S.C. 321-394)). All definitions in section 201 of the act shall apply to these regulations.

(b) **Complaint** means any written, electronic, or oral communication that alleges deficiencies related to the identity, quality, durability, reliability, safety, effectiveness, or performance of a device after it is released for distribution.

(c) **Component** means any raw material, substance, piece, part, software, firmware, labeling, or assembly which is intended to be included as part of the finished, packaged, and labeled device.

(d) **Control number** means any distinctive symbols, such as a distinctive combination of letters or numbers, or both, from which the history of the manufacturing, packaging, labeling, and distribution of a unit, lot, or batch of finished devices can be determined.

(e) **Design history file (DHF)** means a compilation of records which describes the design history of a finished device.

(f) **Design input** means the physical and performance requirements of a device that are used as a basis for device design.

(g) **Design output** means the results of a design effort at each design phase and at the end of the total design effort. The finished design output is the basis for the device master record. The total finished design output consists of the device, its packaging and labeling, and the device master record.

(h) **Design review** means a documented, comprehensive, systematic examination of a design to evaluate the adequacy of the design requirements, to evaluate the capability of the design to meet these requirements, and to identify problems.

(i) **Device history record (DHR)** means a compilation of records containing the production history of a finished device.

(j) **Device master record (DMR)** means a compilation of records containing the procedures and specifications for a finished device.

(k) **Establish** means define, document (in writing or electronically), and implement.

(l) **Finished device** means any device or accessory to any device that is suitable for use or capable of functioning, whether or not it is packaged, labeled, or sterilized.

DEFINITIONS

(m) **Lot or batch** means one or more components or finished devices that consist of a single type, model, class, size, composition, or software version that are manufactured under essentially the same conditions and that are intended to have uniform characteristics and quality within specified limits.

(n) **Management with executive responsibility** means those senior employees of a manufacturer who have the authority to establish or make changes to the manufacturer's quality policy and quality system.

(o) **Manufacturer** means any person who designs, manufactures, fabricates, assembles, or processes a finished device. Manufacturer includes but is not limited to those who perform the functions of contract sterilization, installation, relabeling, remanufacturing, repacking, or specification development, and initial distributor(s) of foreign entities performing these functions.

(p) **Manufacturing material** means any material or substance used in or used to facilitate the manufacturing process, a concomitant constituent, or a byproduct constituent produced during the manufacturing process, which is present in or on the finished device as a residue or impurity not by design or intent of the manufacturer.

(q) **Nonconformity** means the nonfulfillment of a specified requirement.

(r) **Product** means components, manufacturing materials, in-process devices, finished devices, and returned devices.

(s) **Quality** means the totality of features and characteristics that bear on the ability of a device to satisfy fitness-for-use, including safety and performance.

(t) **Quality audit** means a systematic, independent examination of a manufacturer's quality system that is performed at defined intervals and at sufficient frequency to determine whether both quality system activities and the results of such activities comply with quality system procedures, that these procedures are implemented effectively, and that these procedures are suitable to achieve quality system objectives.

(u) **Quality policy** means the overall intentions and direction of an organization with respect to quality, as established by management with executive responsibility.

(v) **Quality system** means the organizational structure, responsibilities, procedures, processes, and resources for implementing quality management.

(w) **Remanufacturer** means any person who processes, conditions, renovates, repackages, restores, or does any other act to a finished device that significantly changes the finished device's performance or safety specifications, or intended use.

(x) **Rework** means action taken on a nonconforming product so that it will fulfill the specified DMR requirements before it is released for distribution.

(y) **Specification** means any requirement with which a product, process, service, or other activity must conform.

(z) **Validation** means confirmation by examination and provision of objective evidence that the particular requirements for a specific intended use can be consistently fulfilled.

(1) **Process validation** means establishing by objective evidence that a process consistently produces a result or product meeting its predetermined specifications.

(2) **Design validation** means establishing by objective evidence that device specifications conform with user needs and intended use(s).

(aa) **Verification** means confirmation by examination and provision of objective evidence that specified requirements have been fulfilled.

1978: § 820.3 DEFINITIONS

 ## ANSI/ISO/ASQC Q9001-1994

3 Definitions

For the purposes of this American National Standard, the definitions given in ISO 8402 and the following definitions apply.

3.1 product: Result of activities or processes.

NOTES

2   A product may include service, hardware, processed materials, software, or a combination thereof.

3   A product can be tangible (e.g., assemblies or processed materials) or intangible (e.g., knowledge or concepts), or a combination thereof.

4 For the purposes of this American National Standard, the term "product" applies to the intended product offering only and not to unintended "by-products" affecting the environment. This differs from the definition given in ISO 8402.

3.2 tender: Offer made by a supplier in response to an invitation to satisfy a contract award to provide product.

3.3 contract; accepted order: Agreed requirements between a supplier and customer transmitted by any means.

ALSO SEE ISO/DIS 13485:1996, 3 DEFINITIONS

 **FDA GUIDANCE**

§ 820.3 Definitions

The term "establish" is only used where documentation is necessary. FDA notes that the quality system regulation is premised on the theory that adequate written procedures, which are implemented appropriately, will likely ensure the safety and effectiveness of the device. ISO 9001:1994 relies on the same premise. The 1994 version of ISO 9001 broadly requires the manufacturer to "establish, document, and maintain a quality system," which includes documenting procedures to meet the requirements.

FDA added the definition of "remanufacturer" to codify its long-standing policy and interpretation of the original CGMP. The language is consistent with the 510(k) provisions and the premarket approval amendment/supplement requirements because FDA has always considered remanufacturers to be manufacturers of a new device.

FDA has adopted the ISO 8402:1994 definition of validation. "Validation" is a step beyond verification to ensure that user needs and intended uses can be fulfilled on a consistent basis. FDA has further distinguished "process validation" from "design validation" to help clarify these two types of validation. The "process validation" definition follows from FDA's *Guidelines on General Principles of Process Validation*. The definition for "design validation" is consistent with the requirements contained in § 820.30, "Design controls." The ISO 8402:1994 definition of "verification" has been adopted. "Verification" is confirmation by examination and provision of objective evidence that specified requirements for a particular device or activity at hand have been met.

NOTES

NOTES

B

Quality System Requirements

FDA QUALITY SYSTEM REGULATION—1996

§ 820.5 Quality systems

Each manufacturer shall establish and maintain a quality system that is appropriate for the specific medical device(s) designed or manufactured, and that meets the requirements of this part.

1978: § 820.5 QUALITY ASSURANCE PROGRAM

ANSI/ISO/ASQC Q9001-1994

4 Quality-system requirements

4.2 Quality system

4.2.1 General

The supplier shall establish, document, and maintain a quality system as a means of ensuring that product conforms to specified requirements. The supplier shall prepare a quality manual covering the requirements of this American National Standard. The quality manual shall include or make reference to the quality-system procedures and outline the structure of the documentation used in the quality system.

NOTE 6 Guidance on quality manuals is given in ISO 10013.

ALSO SEE ISO/DIS 13485:1996, 4.2 QUALITY SYSTEM AND 4.2.1 GENERAL

QUALITY SYSTEMS

 **FDA GUIDANCE**

§ 820.5 Quality system

The broad requirements in § 820.5 are the foundation on which the remaining quality system requirements are built.

 **GHTF GUIDANCE**

4.2 Quality system

4.2.1 General

The implementation of a quality system by the supplier is most effective when those in the organization understand its intention and how it functions, in particular in the area of their responsibility and its interface with other parts of the system.

The quality manual is an essential aid to this understanding by those both inside and outside the supplier's organization. The quality manual could be one document supported by several tiers of documents, each tier becoming progressively more detailed. For example, there may be an overall system manual and one or more specific procedural manuals. Together these documents define the quality system.

NOTE: For general guidance on the content of a quality manual, it is recommended to refer to ISO 10013.

One of the tiers of documents supporting the quality manual is a "Device Master File" or "Device Master Record" (DMR) for each product type (see 4.4.5). This contains, or gives reference to the location of, documentation relevant to the design, manufacture, installation, and servicing of that product. Examples of such documentation may include:

—specifications for raw materials, labels, packaging materials, intermediate and finished products;
—drawings, software design specifications, and source code;
—work instructions (including equipment operation), production methods, environmental specifications;
—sterilization process details (if applicable);
—inspection procedures and acceptance criteria;
—installation and servicing procedures (if applicable).

Such files may also contain quality records (see 4.16) such as:

—design verification records;
—process validation records.

All this documentation forms part of the quality system and should be subject to document control procedures (see 4.5).

FDA QUALITY SYSTEM REGULATION—1996

§ 820.20 Management responsibility

§ 820.20(a) *Quality policy.* Management with executive responsibility shall establish its policy and objectives for, and commitment to, quality. Management with executive responsibility shall ensure that the quality policy is understood, implemented, and maintained at all levels of the organization.

 **ANSI/ISO/ASQC Q9001-1994**

4.1 Management responsibility

4.1.1 Quality policy

The supplier's management with executive responsibility shall define and document its policy for quality, including objectives for quality and its commitment to quality. The quality policy shall be relevant to the supplier's organizational goals and the expectations and needs of its customers. The supplier shall ensure that this policy is understood, implemented, and maintained at all levels of the organization.

 **FDA GUIDANCE**

§ 820.20 Management responsibility

§ 820.20(a) Quality policy

Management with executive responsibility is the level of management that has the authority to establish and make changes to the company quality policy. The establishment of quality objectives, the translation of such objectives into actual methods and procedures, and the implementation of the quality system may be delegated; the regulation does not prohibit delegation. However, it is the responsibility of the highest level of management to establish the quality policy and to ensure that it is followed. (See *United States v. Dotterweich*, 320 U.S. 277 (1943), and *United States v. Park*, 421 U.S. 658 (1975).)

Without question, it is management's responsibility to undertake appropriate actions to ensure that employees understand management's policies and objectives. Understanding is a learning process achieved through training and reinforcement. Management reinforces understanding of policies and objectives by demonstrating a commitment to the quality system visibly and actively on a continuous basis. Such commitment can be demonstrated by providing adequate resources and training to support quality system development and implementation.

GHTF GUIDANCE

4.1 Management responsibility

4.1.1 Quality policy

When defining and documenting its quality policy, quality objectives, and commitment to quality, supplier management should consider the following points:

a.   The quality policy should be expressed in language which is easy to understand.

b.   The quality policy should be relevant to the organization, its other policies, the products or services provided, and the organization's personnel.

c.   The objectives should be achievable.

Management should demonstrate commitment visibly and actively on a continuing basis. Commitment can be demonstrated by activities such as the following:

—ensuring the organization's personnel understand and implement the quality policy;

—initiating, managing, and following up on the implementation of the quality policy, including implementation of the quality system;

—not accepting deviations from quality policy or wasted resources in any part or aspect of the organization.

—providing adequate resources and training to support quality system development and implementation.

FDA QUALITY SYSTEM REGULATION—1996

§ 820.20(b) Organization

Each manufacturer shall establish and maintain an adequate organizational structure to ensure that devices are designed and produced in accordance with the requirements of this part.

§ 820.20(b)(1) *Responsibility and authority.* Each manufacturer shall establish the appropriate responsibility, authority, and interrelation of all personnel who manage, perform, and assess work affecting quality, and provide the independence and authority necessary to perform these tasks.

ANSI/ISO/ASQC Q9001-1994

4.1.2 Organization

4.1.2.1 Responsibility and authority

The responsibility, authority, and the interrelation of personnel who manage, perform, and verify work affecting quality shall be defined and documented, particularly for personnel who need the organizational freedom and authority to:

a)   initiate action to prevent the occurrence of any nonconformities relating to product, process, and quality system;

b)   identify and record any problems relating to the product, process, and quality system;

c)   initiate, recommend, or provide solutions through designated channels;

d)   verify the implementation of solutions;

e)   control further processing, delivery, or installation of nonconforming product until the deficiency or unsatisfactory condition has been corrected.

 **FDA GUIDANCE**

§ 820.20(b) Organization

The organizational structure should ensure that the technical, administrative, and human factors functions affecting the quality of the device will be controlled, whether these functions involve hardware, software, processed materials, or services. All such control should be oriented toward the reduction, elimination, or, ideally, prevention of quality nonconformities. The organizational structure established will be determined in part by the type of device produced, the manufacturer's organizational goals, and the expectations and needs of customers. What may be an adequate organizational structure for manufacturing a relatively simple device may not be adequate for the production of a more complex device, such as a defibrillator.

§ 820.20(b)(1) Responsibility and authority

It is crucial to the success of the quality system for the manufacturer to ensure that responsibility, authority, and organizational freedom (or independence) is provided to those who initiate action to prevent nonconformities; identify and document quality problems; initiate, recommend, provide, and verify solutions to quality problems; and direct or control further processing, delivery, or installation of nonconforming product. Organizational freedom or independence does not necessarily require a stand-alone group, but responsibility, authority, and independence should be sufficient to attain the assigned quality objectives with the desired efficiency.

 **GHTF GUIDANCE**

4.1.2 Organization

4.1.2.1 Responsibility and authority

Individuals in the supplier organization should be aware of the scope, responsibility, and authority of their functions and their impact on product or service quality.

Adequate authority should be delegated to individuals to allow them to carry out their designated responsibilities. They should have clear understanding of their defined authority and freedom, and designated channels to take action. Everyone in the organization should be made aware of the quality objectives and should feel responsibility for achieving them and for fulfilling the requirements for the quality of its products. It is usual to designate one or more individuals to monitor and to report the quality achieved. It is important that those so designated have access to the highest levels of management in the organization.

Responsibilities for key elements of the quality system may be defined in a combination of organization charts and written job descriptions. These key elements include (but are not limited to):

—the control and maintenance of the quality system, aimed at the identification and prevention of quality deficiencies against the specified requirements for the product, process, and quality system;

—the control of a corrective action system that prevents the recurrence of the quality deficiencies, by ensuring that changes to the quality system intended to prevent manufacture of non-conforming product are effective;

—organizing formal and systematic management reviews of the quality system to ensure that it remains appropriate to the quality objectives;

—the expert assessment of any procedures for environmental control and the validation protocols for all processes where environmental control is of significance;

—managerial control of any special processes, and ensuring these operate within validated parameters.

FDA QUALITY SYSTEM REGULATION—1996

§ 820.20(b)(2) Resources

Each manufacturer shall provide adequate resources, including the assignment of trained personnel, for management, performance of work, and assessment activities, including internal quality audits, to meet the requirements of this part.

1978: § 820.20 ORGANIZATION

ANSI/ISO/ASQC Q9001-1994

4.1.2.2 Resources

The supplier shall identify resource requirements and provide adequate resources, including the assignment of trained personnel (see 4.18), for management, performance of work, and verification activities including internal quality audits.

FDA GUIDANCE

§ 820.20(b)(2) Resources

FDA acknowledges that § 820.25(a), "General," requires that sufficiently trained personnel be employed. However, § 820.20(b)(2), "Resources," emphasizes that *all* resource needs must be provided for, including financing, supplies, and personnel. In contrast, § 820.25(a) specifically addresses education, background, training, and experience requirements for personnel.

GHTF GUIDANCE

4.1.2.2 Resources

Supplier management should recognize that adequate resources and personnel can involve the following:

—people doing the management, performance of work, and verification activities;

—awareness of standards and the working arrangements which exist;

—training (see 4.18);

—sufficient time to do the work;

—production schedules which allow time for activities such as inspection, test, and verification;

—equipment;

—documented procedures;

—means to access quality records.

Management may consider obtaining specialist professional advice through a subcontract to another organization, while employing their own staff to implement agreed procedures in a routine manner. In such cases records of the qualifications of the subcontracted personnel should be readily available.

FDA QUALITY SYSTEM REGULATION—1996

§ 820.20(b)(3) Management representative

Management with executive responsibility shall appoint, and document such appointment of, a member of management who, irrespective of other responsibilities, shall have established authority over and responsibility for:

(i) Ensuring that quality system requirements are effectively established and effectively maintained in accordance with this part; and

(ii) Reporting on the performance of the quality system to management with executive responsibility for review.

1978: § 820.20 ORGANIZATION AND § 820.20(a)(4) QUALITY ASSURANCE PROGRAM REQUIREMENTS

 **ANSI/ISO/ASQC Q9001-1994**

4.1.2.3 Management representative

The supplier's management with executive responsibility shall appoint a member of the supplier's own management who, irrespective of other responsibilities, shall have defined authority for

a) ensuring that a quality system is established, implemented, and maintained in accordance with this American National Standard, and

b) reporting on the performance of the quality system to the supplier's management for review and as a basis for improvement of the quality system.

NOTE 5 The responsibility of a management representative may also include liaison with external parties on matters relating to the supplier's quality system.

FDA GUIDANCE

§ 820.20(b)(3) Management representative

When a member of management is appointed to this function, potential conflicts of interest should be examined to ensure that the effectiveness of the quality system is not compromised.

Information collected in complying with §§ 820.20(b)(3)(ii) and 820.100, "Corrective and preventive action," should be used not only for detecting and correcting deficiencies, but also to improve the device and quality system.

GHTF GUIDANCE

4.1.2.3 Management representative

The management representative may have other functions. Where this is the case, the responsibilities and authorities for both the quality system and the other functions should be clearly defined. Potential conflicts of interest should be examined to ensure that the effectiveness of the quality system is not degraded. The organizational structure should show how the position of the management representative is linked with line management in order that the duties of the management representative can be effectively discharged.

   To ensure that the management representative's duties remain clearly defined, he/she alone should be authorized to delegate his/her defined authority.

FDA QUALITY SYSTEM REGULATION—1996

§ 820.20(c) Management review

Management with executive responsibility shall review the suitability and effectiveness of the quality system at defined intervals and with sufficient frequency according to established procedures to ensure that the quality system satisfies the requirements of this part and the manufacturer's established quality policy and objectives. The dates and results of quality system reviews shall be documented.

ANSI/ISO/ASQC Q9001-1994

4.1.3 Management review

The supplier's management with executive responsibility shall review the quality system at defined intervals sufficient to ensure its continuing suitability and effectiveness in satisfying the requirements of this American National Standard and the supplier's stated quality policy and objectives (see 4.1.1). Records of such reviews shall be maintained (see 4.16).

 **FDA GUIDANCE**

§ 820.20(c) Management review

FDA will not request to inspect and copy the reports of reviews required by § 820.20(c) when conducting routine inspections to determine compliance with this part. FDA believes that refraining from routinely reviewing these reports may help ensure that the audits are complete and candid and of maximum use to the manufacturer. FDA does believe, however, that documentation of the dates and results of quality system reviews is important, and FDA may require that management with executive responsibility certify in writing that the manufacturer has complied with the requirements of § 820.20(c).

FDA will also review the written procedures required by § 820.20(c), as well as all other records required under § 820.20. Procedures should require that the review be conducted at appropriate intervals and should be designed to ensure that all parts of the quality system are adequately reviewed. A manufacturer may, of course, develop procedures that permit review of different areas at different times, so long as such reviews are sufficient to carry out the objectives of this section. If there are known problems, for example, a "sufficient frequency" may be fairly frequent. Further, because FDA will not be reviewing the results of such reviews, it must be assured that this function will occur in a consistent manner.

The purpose of the management reviews required by § 820.20(c) is to determine if the manufacturer's quality policy and quality objectives are being met, and to ensure the continued suitability and effectiveness of the quality system. An evaluation of the findings of internal and supplier audits should be included in the § 820.20(c) evaluation. The management review may include a review of the following:

(1) the organizational structure, including the adequacy of staffing and resources;

(2) the quality of the finished device in relation to the quality objectives;

(3) combined information based on purchaser feedback, internal feedback (such as results of internal audits), process performance, and product (including servicing) performance, among other things;

(4) internal audit results and corrective and preventive actions taken.

Management reviews should include considerations for updating the quality system in relation to changes brought about by new technologies, quality concepts, market strategies, and other social or environmental conditions. Management should also review periodically the appropriateness of the review frequency, based on the findings of previous reviews. The quality system review process in § 820.20(c) and the reasons for the review should be understood by the organization.

The requirements under § 820.22, "Quality audit," are for an internal audit and review of the quality system to verify compliance with the quality system regulation. The review and evaluations under § 820.22 are very focused. During the internal quality audit, the manufacturer should review all procedures to ensure adequacy and compliance with the regulation, and determine whether the procedures are being effectively implemented at all times. In contrast, as noted, the management review under § 820.20(c) is a broader review of the organization as a whole to ensure that the quality policy is implemented and the quality objectives are met. The reviews of the quality policy and objectives (§ 820.20(c)) should be carried out by top management, and the review of supporting activities (§ 820.22) should be carried out by management with executive responsibility for quality and other appropriate members of management, utilizing competent personnel as decided on by management.

 **GHTF GUIDANCE**

4.1.3 Management review

Management can fulfill its duty to monitor the continuing suitability and effectiveness of the quality system by conducting periodic, systematic reviews. Such management reviews are additional to, and use the findings of, internal quality audits (see 4.17) conducted to ensure continued adherence to the system. Both management reviews and quality audits should be performed regularly, and not only be conducted as a reaction after quality problems have been identified.

The quality system review process and the reasons behind it should be known and understood by the organization. Reviews may include the following:

—the organizational structure, including the adequacy of staffing and resources;

—the structure and degree of implementation of the quality system;

—the achieved quality of the end product or service in relation to the requirements for quality;

—information based on purchaser feedback, internal feedback (such as results of internal audits), process performance, and product (including services) performance.

The management should review periodically the appropriateness of the review frequency. The frequency depends on individual circumstances. (Some organizations have found that annual management reviews are appropriate, but this interval is not mandatory).

Activities and results may be evaluated on a systemic and/or random basis. Chronic problem areas should receive special attention. Results should be documented and analyzed for trends that may indicate systematic problems.

Required changes to the quality system determined during a management review should be implemented in a timely manner. The effectiveness of any changes should be evaluated.

 ## FDA QUALITY SYSTEM REGULATION—1996

§ 820.20(d) Quality planning

Each manufacturer shall establish a quality plan which defines the quality practices, resources, and activities relevant to devices that are designed and manufactured. The manufacturer shall establish how the requirements for quality will be met.

 ## ANSI/ISO/ASQC Q9001-1994

4.2.3 Quality planning

The supplier shall define and document how the requirements for quality will be met. Quality planning shall be consistent with all other requirements of a supplier's quality system and shall be documented in a format to suit the supplier's method of operation. The supplier shall give consideration to the following activities, as appropriate, in meeting the specified requirements for products, projects, or contracts:

a) the preparation of quality plans;

b) the identification and acquisition of any controls, processes, equipment (including inspection and test equipment), fixtures, resources, and skills that may be needed to achieve the required quality;

c) ensuring the compatibility of the design, the production process, installation, servicing, inspection, and test procedures, and the applicable documentation;

d) the updating, as necessary, of quality control, inspection, and testing techniques, including the development of new instrumentation;

e) the identification of any measurement requirement involving capability that exceeds the known state of the art, in sufficient time for the needed capability to be developed;

f) the identification of suitable verification at appropriate stages in the realization of product;

g) the clarification of standards of acceptability for all features and requirements, including those which contain a subjective element;

h) the identification and preparation of quality records (see 4.16).

NOTE 8 The quality plans referred to (see 4.2.3a) may be in the form of a reference to the appropriate documented procedures that form an integral part of the supplier's quality system.

 **FDA GUIDANCE**

§ 820.20(d) Quality planning

§ 820.20(d) is consistent with ISO 9001:1994, section 4.2.3, "Quality planning."

 **GHTF GUIDANCE**

4.2.3 Quality planning

Quality plans may be used to define how the quality system requirements will be met for a specific class of products. Most of them will have a sequence of activities in relation to a time frame.

Here again the plans can be in several tiers, becoming progressively more detailed. An example could include a detailed sequence of inspections, relating to a product (including service), along with type of inspection equipment and quality record requirements.

NOTE: For general guidance on quality plans it is recommended to refer to ISO 9004-5.

FDA QUALITY SYSTEM REGULATION—1996

§ 820.20(e) Quality system procedures

Each manufacturer shall establish quality system procedures and instructions. An outline of the structure of the documentation used in the quality system shall be established where appropriate.

ANSI/ISO/ASQC Q9001-1994

4.2.2 Quality-system procedures

The supplier shall

a)   prepare documented procedures consistent with the requirements of this American National Standard and the supplier's stated quality policy, and

b)   effectively implement the quality system and its documented procedures.

For the purposes of this American National Standard, the range and detail of the procedures that form part of the quality system shall be dependent upon the complexity of the work, the methods used, and the skills and training needed by personnel involved in carrying out the activity.

NOTE 7 Documented procedures may make reference to work instructions that define how an activity is performed.

FDA GUIDANCE

§ 820.20(e) Quality system procedures

FDA believes that outlining the structure of the documentation is beneficial and, at times, may be critical to the effective operation of the quality system. FDA recognizes, however, that it may not be necessary to create an outline in all cases, for example, with smaller manufacturers and manufacturers of less complicated devices. Thus, the outline is only required where appropriate.

GHTF GUIDANCE

4.2.2 Quality system procedures

Documented procedures should exist which show how each element of the quality system requirements is met. These procedures should reflect the supplier's quality policy and organization and the nature of the product(s) or service(s) being supplied.

The procedures may refer to work instructions that define how an activity is carried out in relation to a specific product, or product type, or service.

FDA QUALITY SYSTEM REGULATION—1996

§ 820.22 Quality audit

Each manufacturer shall establish procedures for quality audits and conduct such audits to assure that the quality system is in compliance with the established quality system requirements and to determine the effectiveness of the quality system.

- Quality audits shall be conducted by individuals who do not have direct responsibility for the matters being audited.
- Corrective action(s), including a reaudit of deficient matters, shall be taken when necessary.
- A report of the results of each quality audit, and reaudit(s) where taken, shall be made and such reports shall be reviewed by management having responsibility for the matters audited.
- The dates and results of quality audits and reaudits shall be documented.

1978: § 820.20(b) AUDIT PROCEDURES

 # ANSI/ISO/ASQC Q9001-1994

4.17 Internal quality audits

The supplier shall establish and maintain documented procedures for planning and implementing internal quality audits to verify whether quality activities and related results comply with planned arrangements and to determine the effectiveness of the quality system.

Internal quality audits shall be scheduled on the basis of the status and importance of the activity to be audited and shall be carried out by personnel independent of those having direct responsibility for the activity being audited.

The results of the audits shall be recorded (see 4.16) and brought to the attention of the personnel having responsibility in the area audited. The management personnel responsible for the area shall take timely corrective action on deficiencies found during the audit.

Follow-up audit activities shall verify and record the implementation and effectiveness of the corrective action taken (see 4.16).

20 The results of internal quality audits form an integral part of the input to management review activities (see 4.1.3).

21 Guidance on quality-system audits is given in ANSI/ISO/ASQC Q10011-1-1994, ANSI/ISO/ASQC Q10011-2-1994, and ANSI/ISO/ASQC Q10011-3-1994.

FDA GUIDANCE

§ 820.22 Quality audit

Manufacturers must realize that conducting effective quality audits is crucial. Without the feedback provided by the quality audit and other information sources, such as complaints and service records, manufacturers operate in an open-loop system with no assurance that the process used to design and produce devices is operating in a state of control.

GHTF GUIDANCE

4.17 Internal quality audits

Internal quality audits as required by ISO 9001 are carried out by the supplier in order to determine whether the various quality system elements of the organization are effective and suitable for achieving the stated quality objectives. The internal audit plan should include the frequency of periodic audits. The supplier should select and assign competent auditors for the activity being audited.

Periodic internal audits are performed:

—to determine the adequacy and conformity of the quality system elements with the requirements for their documentation and implementation requirements;

—to determine the effectiveness of the implemented quality system in meeting the specified quality objectives;

—to meet regulatory requirements;

—to provide an opportunity to improve the supplier's quality system;

—to facilitate external quality assurance.

A well-established system of internal auditing is to examine the different sections of the operation individually and in turn so

QUALITY AUDIT

that the entire operation is covered in the course of a reasonable period. Such a system can be operated flexibly to give special, or repeat, attention to any areas of weakness.

In addition to the periodic internal audits, an internal audit may be initiated for any of the following reasons:

—initially to evaluate the quality system;
—to verify that the quality system continues to meet specified requirements, and is being implemented;
—when significant changes have been made in functional areas, for example, revisions of organizations and procedures which affect quality processes;
—when safety, performance, or dependability of the products (including services) are in, or are suspected to be in, jeopardy due to nonconformities;
—when it is necessary to verify that required corrective actions have been taken, and have been effective;
—when the quality system is evaluated against a quality system standard.

Target dates for responding to audit observations should be established.

Only records which demonstrate that an effective internal audit system is in operation need to be made available to third-party auditors. This may be done by:

—providing documented procedures for the conduct of audits;
—providing audit schedules;
—demonstrating that internal audits have been performed;
—demonstrating that corrective actions have been initiated and completed.

NOTE: For general guidelines for auditing quality systems it is recommended to refer to ISO 10011-1, ISO 10011-2 and ISO 10011-3, but the guidance in ISO 10011 Parts 1, 2, 3 does not add to, or otherwise change, the requirements of ISO 9001.

QUALITY AUDIT

§ 820.25 Personnel

§ 820.25(a) *General.* Each manufacturer shall have sufficient personnel with the necessary education, background, training, and experience to assure that all activities required by this part are correctly performed.

1978: § 820.25 PERSONNEL

§ 820.25(b) Training

Each manufacturer shall establish procedures for identifying training needs and ensure that all personnel are trained to adequately perform their assigned responsibilities. Training shall be documented.

(1) As part of their training, personnel shall be made aware of device defects which may occur from the improper performance of their specific jobs.

(2) Personnel who perform verification and validation activities shall be made aware of defects and errors that may be encountered as part of their job functions.

1978: § 820.25(a) PERSONNEL TRAINING

 ANSI/ISO/ASQC Q9001-1994

4.18 Training

The supplier shall establish and maintain documented procedures for identifying training needs and provide for the training of all personnel performing activities affecting quality. Personnel performing specific assigned tasks shall be qualified on the basis of appropriate education, training, and/or experience, as required. Appropriate records of training shall be maintained (see 4.16).

 **FDA GUIDANCE**

§ 820.25 Personnel

Whether sufficient personnel are employed will be determined by the requirements of the quality system, which must be designed to ensure that the requirements of the regulation are properly implemented. In making staffing decisions, a manufacturer must ensure that persons assigned to particular functions are properly equipped and possess the necessary education, background, training, and experience to perform their functions correctly. The manufacturer must determine for itself what constitutes "sufficient" personnel with proper qualification in the first instance.

§ 820.25(b) Training

The training procedure must include the identification of training needs. A training program to ensure that personnel adequately perform their assigned responsibilities also should include information about the CGMP requirements and how particular job functions relate to the overall quality system. It is imperative that training cover the consequences of improper performance so that personnel know what defects to look for, as well as be aware of the effect their actions can have on the safety and effectiveness of the device. In order for the full quality system to function as intended, all personnel should be properly trained. Each function in the manufacture of a medical device must be viewed as integral to all other functions.

 **GHTF GUIDANCE**

4.18 Training

The training of personnel in an organization is essential for the achievement of quality objectives. This includes specific training necessary for performing assigned tasks and general training both to build incentives and to heighten quality awareness. Personnel should be trained in the usage of, and the underlying reasons for, the procedures and documents in the quality management approach of the supplier.

Training should be given as an introduction to new employees and for all personnel engaged in work affecting quality at intervals, and should:

—include the intended use of the products;

—identify quality problems which could arise from the inadequate or improper performance of the specified tasks;

—describe any specific hygiene requirements;

—include instruction on conduct to avoid jeopardizing the integrity of special environmental conditions, when applicable;

—include, when appropriate, procedures to be followed on receipt of customer feedback.

To achieve and maintain proficiency a number of steps can periodically be taken by the supplier as follows:

—evaluation of the general education, experience, and proficiency of the personnel for the activities to be performed;

—identification of the individual training needs against those required for satisfactory performance;

—planning, organization, and conduct of appropriate training, either in-house or by an outside body;

—recording of training and achievement so that records can be updated and gaps in training can readily be identified and filled.

NOTES

NOTES

SUBPART C
Design Controls

FDA QUALITY SYSTEM REGULATION—1996

§ 820.30 Design controls

§ 820.30(a) *General.* (1) Each manufacturer of any class III or class II device, and the class I devices listed in paragraph (a)(2) of this section, shall establish and maintain procedures to control the design of the device in order to ensure that specified design requirements are met.

(2) The following class I devices are subject to design controls:

(i) Devices automated with computer software; and

(ii) The devices listed in the chart below.

Section	Device
868.6810	Catheter, Tracheobronchial Suction
878.4460	Glove, Surgeon's
880.6760	Restraint, Protective
892.5650	System, Applicator, Radionuclide, Manual
892.5740	Source, Radionuclide Teletherapy

ANSI/ISO/ASQC Q9001-1994

4.4 Design control

4.4.1 General

The supplier shall establish and maintain documented procedures to control and verify the design of the product in order to ensure that the specified requirements are met.

 **FDA GUIDANCE**

§ 820.30 Design controls

Since early 1984, FDA has identified lack of design controls as one of the major causes of device recalls. The intrinsic quality of devices, including their safety and effectiveness, is established during the design phase. Thus, FDA believes that unless appropriate design controls are observed during preproduction stages of development, a finished device may be neither safe nor effective for its intended use. The SMDA provided FDA with the authority to add preproduction design controls to the device CGMP regulation. Based on its experience with administering the original CGMP regulation, which did not include preproduction design controls, the agency was concerned that the original regulation provided less than an adequate level of assurance that devices would be safe and effective. Therefore, FDA has added general requirements for design controls to the device CGMP regulation for all class III and II devices and certain class I devices. FDA is not subjecting the majority of class I devices to design controls because it does not believe that such controls are necessary to ensure that such devices are safe and effective and otherwise in compliance with the act. However, all devices, including class I devices exempt from design controls, must be properly transferred to production in order to comply with § 820.181, as well as other applicable requirements. For most class I devices, FDA believes that the production and other controls in the new quality system regulation and other general controls of the act will be sufficient, as they have been in the past, to ensure safety and effectiveness.

The design control requirements are not intended to apply to the development of concepts and feasibility studies. Once it is decided that a design will be developed, however, a plan must be established to determine the adequacy of the design requirements and to ensure that the design that will eventually be released to production meets the approved requirements.

Those who design medical devices must be aware of the design control requirements in the regulation and comply with them. Unsafe and ineffective devices are often the result of informal development that does not ensure the proper establishment and assessment of design requirements that are necessary to develop a medical device that is safe and effective for the intended use of the device and that meets the needs of the user.

FDA investigators will not inspect a device under the design control requirements to determine whether the design is appropriate or "safe and effective." Section 520(f)(1)(a) of the act precludes FDA from evaluating the "safety or effectiveness of a device" through preproduction design control procedures. FDA investigators will evaluate the process, the methods, and the procedures that a manufacturer has established to implement the requirements for design controls. If, based on any information gained during an inspection, an investigator believes that distributed devices are unsafe or ineffective, the investigator has an obligation to report the observations to the Center for Devices and Radiological Health (CDRH).

 **GHTF GUIDANCE**

4.4 Design control

4.4.1 General

The essential quality aspects and the regulatory requirements, such as safety, performance, and dependability of a product (whether hardware, software, services, or processed materials), are established during the design and development phase. Deficient design can be a major cause of quality problems. ISO 9001 specifies design control requirements for the design process. In considering design control, it is important to note that the design function may apply to various facets of the operation in differing styles and time scales. Such facets are related to products, including services and software, as well as to process design associated with product design. The supplier should consider all phases of the design associated with product design. The supplier should consider all phases of the design function process for which controlled procedures are necessary.

The nature of product evaluations, design reviews, process validations, etc., should be proportional to the nature of the risks of the device. Use of techniques such as fault tree analysis and failure mode and effects analysis can be helpful in determining the nature of possible design flaws and the risks that they entail.

FDA QUALITY SYSTEM REGULATION—1996

§ 820.30(b) Design and development planning

Each manufacturer shall establish and maintain plans that describe or reference the design and development activities and define responsibility for implementation.

- The plans shall identify and describe the interfaces with different groups or activities that provide, or result in, input to the design and development process.
- The plans shall be reviewed, updated, and approved as design and development evolves.

 ## ANSI/ISO/ASQC Q9001-1994

4.4.2 Design and development planning

The supplier shall prepare plans for each design and development activity. The plans shall describe or reference these activities, and define responsibility for their implementation. The design and development activities shall be assigned to qualified personnel equipped with adequate resources. The plans shall be updated, as the design evolves.

4.4.3 Organizational and technical interfaces

Organizational and technical interfaces between different groups which input into the design process shall be defined and the necessary information documented, transmitted, and regularly reviewed.

 ## FDA GUIDANCE

§ 820.30(b) Design and development planning

§ 820.30(b) requires the plan to describe or reference design activities and define responsibility for implementing the activities, rather than requiring that the plan identify each person responsible for carrying out each activity. FDA notes that § 820.20(b)(1) requires manufacturers to establish the appropriate responsibility for activities affecting quality and emphasizes that the assignment of specific responsibility is important to the success of the design control program and to achieving compliance with the regulation. Also, the design and development activities should be assigned to qualified personnel equipped with adequate resources as required under § 820.20(b)(2).

The plan must identify and describe the interfaces with different groups or activities that provide, or result in, input to the design process. Many organization functions, both inside and outside the design group, may contribute to the design process. For example, interfaces with marketing, purchasing, regulatory affairs, manufacturing, service groups, or information systems may be necessary during the design development phase. To function effectively, the design plan must establish the roles of these groups in the design process and describe the information that should be received and transmitted. A design plan typically includes at least proposed quality practices, assessment methodology, record-keeping and documentation requirements, and resources, as well as a sequence of events related to a particular design or design category. These may be modified and refined as the design evolves. The design process can become a lengthy and costly process if the design activity is not properly defined and planned. The more specifically the activities are defined up front, the less need there will be for changes as the design evolves.

 **GHTF GUIDANCE**

4.4.2 Design and development planning

The design process may become a lengthy and costly process if the design activity is not properly defined and planned.

The supplier's procedures for design and development planning should include such elements as:

—sequential and parallel work schedules with the time scales;

—design verification activities;

—plans for evaluating the safety, performance, and dependability incorporated in the product design;

—plans for methods of product measurement, test, and acceptance criteria;

—assignment of responsibilities.

The design plan typically includes the specific quality practices, assessment methodology, record-keeping, documentation requirements, resources, etc., and sequence of activities relevant to a particular design or design category. The plan should reference applicable codes, standards, regulations, and specifications. However, the plan should only be as comprehensive as needed to meet the quality objectives.

If any clinical evaluation is necessary, the supplier should consider whether any special documentation is required to comply with regulatory procedures.

The supplier should clearly assign responsibilities for specific design leadership and other design work functions to designated personnel. The personnel in these functions should be qualified and have access to information and the resources to complete the work.

Design activities should be specified at the level of detail necessary for carrying out the design process and in a manner which permits verification that the design meets the requirements.

4.4.3 Organizational and technical interfaces

When input to the design is from a variety of sources, their interrelationships and interfaces (as well as the pertinent responsibilities and authorities) should be defined, documented, coordinated, and controlled.

Many organizational functions contribute to the design process. These may include:

—research and development;

—marketing;

—purchasing;

—quality assurance and quality management;

—engineering;

—regulatory affairs;

—materials technology;

—production/manufacturing;

—service groups;

—facilities management;

—warehousing/transportation/logistics;

—communications facilities;

—information systems.

To function effectively, the suppliers' design work groups, both internal and external, should establish:

—what information should be received and transmitted;

—identification of sending and receiving groups;

—the purpose of the information transmittal;

—identification of transmittal mechanisms;

—document transmittal records to be maintained.

FDA QUALITY SYSTEM REGULATION—1996

§ 820.30(c) Design input

Each manufacturer shall establish and maintain procedures to ensure that the design requirements relating to a device are appropriate and address the intended use of the device, including the needs of the user and patient.

- The procedures shall include a mechanism for addressing incomplete, ambiguous, or conflicting requirements.
- The design input requirements shall be documented and shall be reviewed and approved by a designated individual(s).
- The approval, including the date and signature of the individual(s) approving the requirements, shall be documented.

 ANSI/ISO/ASQC Q9001-1994

4.4.4 Design input

Design-input requirements relating to the product, including applicable statutory and regulatory requirements, shall be identified, documented, and their selection reviewed by the supplier for adequacy. Incomplete, ambiguous, or conflicting requirements shall be resolved with those responsible for imposing these requirements.

Design input shall take into consideration the results of any contract-review activities.

 **FDA GUIDANCE**

§ 820.30(c) Design input

This section requires the manufacturer to ensure that the design input requirements are appropriate so the device will perform to meet its intended use and the needs of the user. In doing this, the manufacturer must define the performance characteristics, safety and reliability requirements, environmental requirements and limitations, physical characteristics, applicable standards and regulatory requirements, and labeling and packaging requirements, among other things, and refine the design requirements as verification and validation results are established.

For example, when designing a device, the manufacturer should conduct appropriate human factors studies, analyses, and tests from the early stages of the design process until that point in development at which the interfaces with the medical professional and the patient are fixed. The human interface includes both the hardware and software characteristics that affect device use, and good design is crucial to logical, straightforward, and safe device operation. The human factors methods used (for instance, task/function analyses, user studies, prototype tests, mock-up reviews, and so on) should ensure that the characteristics of the user population and operating environment are considered. In addition, the compatibility of system components should be assessed. Identifying and establishing the environmental limits for safe and effective device operation is inherent in the requirements for ensuring that a device is appropriate for its intended use. Some factors that must be considered when establishing inputs include, where applicable, a determination of energy (for example, electrical, heat, and electromagnetic fields), biological effects (for example, toxicity and biocompatibility), and environmental effects (for example, electromagnetic interference and electrostatic discharge). Finally, labeling (instructions for use) should be tested for usability.

It is important that incomplete, ambiguous, or conflicting requirements be resolved with those responsible for imposing these requirements. Further, it is important that the design input be assessed as early as possible in the development process, making this an ideal time in the device's design development to have a design review to "approve" the design input.

 **GHTF GUIDANCE**

4.4.4 Design input

Design inputs are typically in the form of:

—product description specifications, and/or

—product description with specifications relating to configuration, composition, incorporated elements, and other design features.

All pertinent design inputs (such as performance, functional, descriptive, environmental, safety, quality assurance, and regulatory requirements) should be defined, reviewed, and recorded by the supplier in a design description document(s).

This design description document should quantify all requirements wherever practicable. It lays the foundation and provides a unified approach to the design. It also records the resolutions of any incomplete, ambiguous, or conflicting requirements which have been uncovered.

The design description document should identify those design aspects, materials, and processes which may require development and analysis, including prototype testing to verify their adequacy. The design description document should be prepared in a way that facilitates periodic updates. It should also indicate "when" and "what criteria" will cause the document to be updated, and who is responsible for the update. A design description document prepared in this way serves as the definitive up-to-date reference document as the design progresses to completion.

The specified requirements for medical devices placed on the market are normally set by the supplier, usually based on his perception of clinical need and the potential market. Design input data may also include advice from an appropriately qualified practitioner. For example, consideration may need to be given to anatomical and physiological implications of the intended use of the product. In developing the specified requirements, the supplier should consider other likely uses of the device and the needs for labels and customer training.

The design transfer process (see 4.4.5) will flow more smoothly if, during design input, consideration is given to production (parts and materials availability, equipment needs, training, etc.) and assessment requirements (conformance assessment procedures, methods, and equipment).

 ## FDA QUALITY SYSTEM REGULATION—1996

§ 820.30(d) Design output

Each manufacturer shall establish and maintain procedures for defining and documenting design output in terms that allow an adequate evaluation of conformance to design input requirements.

- Design output procedures shall contain or make reference to acceptance criteria and shall ensure that those design outputs that are essential for the proper functioning of the device are identified.

- Design output shall be documented, reviewed, and approved before release.
- The approval, including the date and signature of the individual(s) approving the output, shall be documented.

ANSI/ISO/ASQC Q9001-1994

4.4.5 Design output

Design output shall be documented and expressed in terms that can be verified against design-input requirements and validated (see 4.4.8).

Design output shall:

a) meet the design-input requirements;

b) contain or make reference to acceptance criteria;

c) identify those characteristics of the design that are crucial to the safe and proper functioning of the product (e.g., operating, storage, handling, maintenance, and disposal requirements).

Design-output documents shall be reviewed before release.

FDA GUIDANCE

§ 820.30(d) Design output

Design outputs are the design specifications that should meet design input requirements, as confirmed during design verification and validation and ensured during design review. Output includes the device, its labeling and packaging, associated specifications and drawings, and production and quality assurance specifications and procedures. These documents are the basis for the device master record (DMR). The total finished design output consists of the device, its labeling and packaging, and the DMR.

Design output can be released or transferred to the next design phase at various stages in the design process, as defined in the design and development plan. The design output is reviewed and approved before release or transfer to the next design phase or production. The design output requirements are intended to apply to all such stages of the design process.

 GHTF GUIDANCE

4.4.5 Design output

Throughout the design process, the requirements contained in the design description are translated by the supplier into outputs, such as the following:

—drawings;
—specifications (including process and material specifications);
—work instructions;
—software;
—quality assurance procedures;
—installation and servicing procedures;
—packaging and labeling specifications, including copies of approved labels, methods, and processes used.

Outputs of the detailed design are the final technical documents used for purchasing, production, installation, inspection and testing, and servicing.

This information, or reference to the location of this information, constitutes the Device Master Record (DMR) (see 4.2).

As part of, or in addition to, the DMR documents, it is good practice to maintain a file to demonstrate that each design was developed and verified in accordance with the approved design plan. Such a file includes or refers to the location of design documentation such as design input requirements, design verification results, design review results, etc.

The DMR should normally be held (or be reasonably accessible) at each site where the product is manufactured. The design file (if separate) need be held only at the design site.

 FDA QUALITY SYSTEM REGULATION—1996

§ 820.30(e) Design review

Each manufacturer shall establish and maintain procedures to ensure that formal documented reviews of the design results are planned and conducted at appropriate stages of the device's design development.

- The procedures shall ensure that participants at each design review include representatives of all functions concerned with the design stage being reviewed and an individual(s) who does not have direct responsibility for the design stage being reviewed, as well as any specialists needed.

- The results of a design review, including identification of the design, the date, and the individual(s) performing the review, shall be documented in the design history file.

ANSI/ISO/ASQC Q9001-1994

4.4.6 Design review

At appropriate stages of design, formal documented reviews of the design results shall be planned and conducted. Participants at each design review shall include representatives of all functions concerned with the design stage being reviewed, as well as other specialist personnel, as required. Records of such reviews shall be maintained (see 4.16).

FDA GUIDANCE

§ 820.30(e) Design review

The purpose of conducting design reviews during the design phase is to ensure that the design satisfies the design input requirements for the intended use of the device and the needs of the user. Design review includes the review of design verification data to determine whether the design outputs meet functional and operational requirements, the design is compatible with components and other accessories, the safety requirements are achieved, the reliability and maintenance requirements are met, the labeling and other regulatory requirements are met, and the manufacturing, installation, and servicing requirements are compatible with the design specifications. Design reviews should be conducted at major decision points throughout the design phase.

Design review provides an opportunity for all those who may have an impact on the quality of the device to provide input, including manufacturing, quality assurance, purchasing, sales, and servicing divisions. While small manufacturers may not have the broad range of disciplines found in a large company, and the need to coordinate and control technical interfaces may be lessened, the principles of design review still apply. The requirements under § 820.30(e) allow small manufacturers to tailor a design review that is appropriate to their individual needs.

Design reviews must be conducted at appropriate stages of design development, which must be defined in the established design and development plan. The number of design reviews will depend on the plan and the complexity of the device. The results of a design review must include identification of the design, the date, and the individual(s) performing the review. Thus, multiple reviews can occur and the manufacturer must document what is being reviewed, when, and by whom.

The requirement states that the procedures shall ensure that each design review includes an individual(s) who does not have direct responsibility for the design stage being reviewed. This requirement will provide an objective view from someone not working directly on that particular part of the design project to ensure that the requirements are met. It is not FDA's intention to prohibit those directly responsible for the design from participating in the design review.

 **GHTF GUIDANCE**

4.4.6 Design review

Design reviews typically are the coordinating design control measure. Design review and/or type testing by an authorized external organization may be a regulatory requirement for certain types of product.

The competence of the participants in the design reviews should be adequate to permit them to examine designs and their implications. Design reviews for the purpose of design verification can consider questions such as the following:

a.   Do designs satisfy all specified requirements for the product (including service)?

b.   Are product design and processing capabilities compatible?

c.   Has a risk analysis been carried out to ensure that safety considerations are covered?

d.   Do designs meet functional and operational requirements, that is, performance and dependability objectives?

e.   Have appropriate materials and/or facilities been selected?

f.   Is there adequate compatibility of materials and components and/or service elements?

g.   Is the design satisfactory for all anticipated environmental and load conditions?

h.   Are components or service elements standardized and do they provide for interchangeability, maintainability, and replacement?

i.   Are plans for implementing the design, for example, purchasing, production, installation, inspection and testing, technically feasible?

j.   Can the tolerance requirements consistently be met?

k.   Where computer software forms part of the product, or has been used in design computations, modeling, or analyses, has the software (and its configuration control) been appropriately validated, authorized, and verified?

l.   Have the inputs to such software, and the outputs, been appropriately verified and documented?

m. What are the assumptions made during the design process and what is their validity?

Records of design review meetings should be retained. The records should identify those present at the meeting and the decisions reached.

FDA QUALITY SYSTEM REGULATION—1996

§ 820.30(f) Design verification

Each manufacturer shall establish and maintain procedures for verifying the device design.

- Design verification shall confirm that the design output meets the design input requirements.
- The results of the design verification, including identification of the design, method(s), the date, and the individual(s) performing the verification, shall be documented in the design history file.

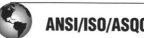

ANSI/ISO/ASQC Q9001-1994

4.4.7 Design verification

At appropriate stages of design, design verification shall be performed to ensure that the design-stage output meets the design-stage input requirements. The design-verification measures shall be recorded (see 4.16).

NOTE 10 In addition to conducting design reviews (see 4.4.6), design verification may include activities such as

—performing alternative calculations,
—comparing the new design with a similar proven design, if available,
—undertaking tests and demonstrations, and
—reviewing the design-stage documents before release.

FDA GUIDANCE

§ 820.30(f) Design verification

Design verification is the testing required to determine whether the design outputs meet functional and operational requirements or design inputs.

GHTF GUIDANCE

4.4.7 Design verification

ISO 9001 describes design control measures (e.g., alternative calculations, tests and demonstrations, comparison with a proven design) which can be used in conjunction with design reviews to verify the design. Design verification should ideally involve personnel other than those responsible for the design work under review.

Once the design is translated into physical form, its safety, performance, and reliability should be verified by testing under simulated use conditions. Such verification may include in-vitro and in-vivo testing.

When alternative calculations or comparison with a proven design are employed as forms of design verification, the appropriateness of the alternative calculation method and/or the proven design should be reviewed in relation to this new application.

FDA QUALITY SYSTEM REGULATION—1996

§ 820.30(g) Design validation

Each manufacturer shall establish and maintain procedures for validating the device design.

* Design validation shall be performed under defined operating conditions on initial production units, lots, or batches, or their equivalents.
* Design validation shall ensure that devices conform to defined user needs and intended uses and shall include testing of production units under actual or simulated use conditions.
* Design validation shall include software validation and risk analysis, where appropriate.
* The results of the design validation, including identification of the design, method(s), the date, and the individual(s) performing the validation, shall be documented in the design history file.

1978: § 820.160 FINISHED DEVICE INSPECTION

 **ANSI/ISO/ASQC Q9001-1994**

4.4.8 Design validation

Design validation shall be performed to ensure that product conforms to defined user needs and/or requirements.

NOTES

11 Design validation follows successful design verification (see 4.4.7).

12 Validation is normally performed under defined operating conditions.

13 Validation is normally performed on the final product, but may be necessary in earlier stages prior to product completion.

14 Multiple validations may be performed if there are different intended uses.

ALSO SEE ISO/DIS 13485:1996, 4.4 DESIGN CONTROL, 4.4.1 GENERAL, AND 4.4.8 DESIGN VALIDATION

 **FDA GUIDANCE**

§ 820.30(g) Design validation

It is important to note that design validation follows successful design verification. Certain aspects of design validation can be accomplished during the design verification, but design verification is not a substitute for design validation. Design validation should be performed under defined operating conditions and on the initial production units, lots, or batches, or their equivalents to ensure proper overall design control and proper design transfer.

When equivalent devices are used in the final design validation, the manufacturer must document in detail how the device was manufactured and how the manufacturing is similar to and possibly different from initial production. Where there are differences, the manufacturer must justify why design validation results are valid for the production units, lots, or batches.

Manufacturers should not use prototypes developed in the laboratory or machine shop as test units to meet these requirements. Prototypes may differ from the finished production devices. During research and development, conditions for building prototypes are typically better controlled and personnel more knowledgeable about what needs to be done and how to do it than are regular production personnel. When going from laboratory to scale-up production, standards, methods, and procedures may not be properly transferred, or additional manufacturing processes may be added. Often, changes not reflected in the prototype are made in the device to facilitate the manufacturing process, and these may adversely affect device functioning and user interface characteristics. Proper testing of devices that are produced using the same methods and procedures as those to be used in routine production will prevent the distribution and subsequent recall of many unacceptable medical devices.

In addition, finished devices must be tested for performance under actual conditions of use or simulated use conditions in the actual or simulated environment in which the device is expected to be used. Simulated use testing samples must be taken from units, lots, or batches that were produced using the same specifications, production and quality system methods, procedures, and equipment that will be used for routine production. FDA considers this a critical element of the design validation. The requirement to conduct simulated use testing of finished devices is found in the original CGMP in § 820.160 as part of finished device inspection. This requirement has been moved to § 820.30(g) because FDA believes that simulated use testing at this point is more effective in ensuring that only safe and effective devices are produced.

Manufacturers must also conduct such tests when they make changes in the device design or the manufacturing process that could affect safety or effectiveness as required in the original CGMP in § 820.100(a)(2). The extent of testing conducted should be governed by the risk(s) the device will present if it fails. FDA considers these activities essential for ensuring that the manufacturing process does not adversely affect the device.

When conducting a risk analysis, manufacturers are expected to identify possible hazards associated with the design in both normal and fault conditions. The risks associated with the hazards, including those resulting from user error, should then be calculated in both normal and fault conditions. If any risk is judged unacceptable, it should be reduced to acceptable levels by the appropriate means, for example, by redesign or warnings. An important part of risk analysis is ensuring that changes made to eliminate or minimize hazards do not introduce new hazards. Tools for conducting such analyses include failure mode effect analysis and fault tree analysis, among others. Risk analysis must be conducted for the majority of devices subject to design controls and is considered to be an essential requirement for medical devices under this regulation, as well as under ISO/CD 13485 and EN 46001. FDA has replaced the phrase "where applicable" with "where appropriate" for consistency with the rest of the regulation.

Design validation may also be necessary in earlier stages, prior to product completion, and multiple validations may need to be performed if there are different intended uses. Proper design validation cannot occur without following all the requirements set forth in the design control section of the regulation.

 **GHTF GUIDANCE**

4.4.8 Design validation

Design validation goes beyond the purely technical issues of verifying that the design output meets the design input, and is intended to ensure that the product meets user requirements. This may involve consideration of who the user really is, the operating instructions, and any restriction on the use of the product.

Clinical evaluation may be involved in the validation of the design of medical devices. The conduct of clinical investigations should conform to applicable regulations/standards.

FDA QUALITY SYSTEM REGULATION—1996

§ 820.30(h) Design transfer

Each manufacturer shall establish and maintain procedures to ensure that the device design is correctly translated into production specifications.

1978: § 820.100 MANUFACTURING SPECIFICATIONS AND PROCESSES AND § 820.100(a)(1) SPECIFICATION CONTROLS

 **FDA GUIDANCE**

§ 820.30(h) Design transfer

Section 820.30(h) now contains a general requirement for the establishment of procedures to ensure that the design basis for the device is correctly translated into production methods and procedures. This is the same requirement that is contained in § 820.100(a) of the original CGMP regulation.

 **GHTF GUIDANCE**

4.4.5 Design transfer

The transfer of a design to production typically involves review and approval of specifications and procedures and, where applicable, the proving of the adequacy of the specification, methods, and procedures through process validation including the testing of finished product under actual or simulated use conditions.

It may not be possible to determine the adequacy of full-scale manufacturing on the basis of successfully building prototypes or models in a laboratory and testing these prototypes or models. The engineering feasibility and production feasibility may be different because the equipment, tools, personnel, operating procedures, supervision, and motivation may be different when a company scales up for routine production. One way to ensure that distributed devices have the quality attributes established during the design phase, and that these are not adversely affected by the production process, is to manufacture finished devices using the approved specifications, the same materials and components, the same production and assessment equipment, and the same meth-

69

ods and procedures that will be used for routine production. Where appropriate, this may be accomplished by manufacturing "pilot runs" or "first production runs."

These devices, or samples from these runs, are then qualified through testing under actual or simulated use conditions, and in the environment (or simulated environment) in which the device is expected to be used. The extent of the testing conducted should be governed by the risk the device will present to the user should it fail and the level of scientific knowledge.

FDA QUALITY SYSTEM REGULATION—1996

§ 820.30(i) Design changes

Each manufacturer shall establish and maintain procedures for the identification, documentation, validation or where appropriate verification, review, and approval of design changes before their implementation.

1978: § 820.100(a)(2) SPECIFICATION CONTROLS

ANSI/ISO/ASQC Q9001-1994

4.4.9 Design changes

All design changes and modifications shall be identified, documented, reviewed, and approved by authorized personnel before their implementation.

FDA GUIDANCE

§ 820.30(i) Design changes

Manufacturers are not expected to maintain records of all changes proposed during the very early stages of the design process; however, all design changes made after the design review that approves the initial design inputs for incorporation into the design, and those changes made to correct design deficiencies once the design has been released to production, must be documented. The records of these changes create a history of the evolution of the design, which can be invaluable for failure investigation and for facilitating the design of future similar products. Such records can prevent the repetition of errors and the development of unsafe or ineffective designs. The evaluation and documentation should be in direct proportion to the significance of the change. Procedures must ensure that after the design requirements are established and approved, changes to the design, both preproduction and postproduction are also reviewed, validated (or verified where appropriate), and approved. Otherwise, a device may be rendered unable to properly perform, and unsafe and ineffective.

The safety and effectiveness of devices cannot be proven by final inspection or testing. Product development is inherently an evolutionary process. While change is a healthy and necessary part of product development, quality can be ensured only if change is controlled and documented in the development process and the production process. Again, manufacturers are not expected to maintain records of changes made during the very early stages of product development; only those design changes made after the approval of the design inputs need to be documented. Each manufacturer must establish criteria for evaluating changes to ensure that the changes are appropriate for its designs.

Note that when a change is made to a specification, method, or procedure, each manufacturer should evaluate the change in accordance with an established procedure to determine if the submission of a premarket notification (510(k)) under § 807.81(a)(3) (21 CFR 807.81(a)(3)) or the submission of a supplement to a PMA under § 814.39(a) (21 CFR 814.39) is required. Records of this evaluation and its results should be maintained.

 **GHTF GUIDANCE**

4.4.9 Design changes

The design of a product may be changed or modified for a number of reasons, for example:

—omissions or errors (e.g., due to calculation, material selection, etc.) during the design phase have been identified afterward;

—manufacturing and/or installation difficulties are discovered after the design phase;

—the purchaser or subcontractor requests changes;

—the function or performance of a product or service is to be improved;

—safety, regulatory, or other requirements have been changed;

—design verification necessitates change (cf. Clause 4.4.7);

—corrective action necessitates change (cf. Clause 4.14).

Changes during the design phase may require change to the design input (4.4.4). The design input should be regarded as a controlled document and any such changes should be made in accordance with the document change procedures (4.5.2).

All design changes should be reviewed to determine whether they influence previously approved design verification results. Design changes in one component of a product should be evaluated for their influence on the whole. Improving one characteristic may have unforeseen adverse influence on another.

When significant design changes are made, the verification procedures (4.4.7) should also be reviewed and modified as appropriate.

Procedures should be established to communicate the new design output (4.4.5) to all concerned, to record any design changes, and to ensure, as well as document, that only authorized design changes have been made.

When the design of a medical device which has already been placed on the market is changed, the supplier should consider whether the regulatory authorities should be notified.

 ## FDA QUALITY SYSTEM REGULATION—1996

§ 820.30(j) Design history file

Each manufacturer shall establish and maintain a design history file for each type of device. The design history file shall contain or reference the records necessary to demonstrate that the design was developed in accordance with the approved design plan and the requirements of this part.

 ## FDA GUIDANCE

§ 820.30(j) Design history file (DHF)

The DMR contains the documentation necessary to produce a device. The final design output from the design phase, which is maintained or referenced in the DHF, will form the basis or starting point for the DMR. Thus, those outputs must be referred to or placed in the DMR. The total finished design output includes the final device, its labeling and packaging, and the DMR that includes device specifications and drawings, as well as all instructions and procedures for production, installation, maintenance, and servicing. The DHF, in contrast, contains or references all the records necessary to establish compliance with the design plan and the regulation, including the design control procedures. The DHF illustrates the history of the design and is necessary so that manufacturers can exercise control over and be accountable for the design process, thereby maximizing the probability that the finished design conforms to the design specifications.

The intent of the DHF is to document, or reference the documentation of, the activities carried out to meet the design plan and requirements of § 820.30. A DHF is, therefore, necessary for each type of device developed. The DHF must provide documentation showing the actions taken with regard to each type of device designed, not generically link devices together with different design characteristics and give a general overview of how the output was reached.

The complete history of the design process should be documented in the DHF. Such records are necessary to ensure that the final design conforms to the design specifications. Depending on the design, that may be relatively few records. Manufacturers who do not document all their efforts may lose the information and experience of those efforts, thereby possibly requiring activities to be duplicated.

NOTES

NOTES

NOTES

Document Controls

FDA QUALITY SYSTEM REGULATION—1996

§ 820.40 Document controls

Each manufacturer shall establish and maintain procedures to control all documents that are required by this part. The procedures shall provide for the following:

ANSI/ISO/ASQC Q9001-1994

4.5 Document and data control

4.5.1 General

The supplier shall establish and maintain documented procedures to control all documents and data that relate to the requirements of this American National Standard including, to the extent applicable, documents of external origin such as standards and customer drawings.

NOTE 15 Documents and data can be in the form of any type of media, such as hard copy or electronic media.

GHTF GUIDANCE

4.5 Document and data control

4.5.1 General

Documents and data containing information and/or instructions can be recorded, transmitted, or received using a variety of media, such as hard copy or electronic media.

FDA QUALITY SYSTEM REGULATION—1996

§ 820.40(a) Document approval and distribution

Each manufacturer shall designate an individual(s) to review for adequacy and approve prior to issuance all documents established to meet the requirements of this part.

- The approval, including the date and signature of the individual(s) approving the document, shall be documented.
- Documents established to meet the requirements of this part shall be available at all locations for which they are designated, used, or otherwise necessary, and all obsolete documents shall be promptly removed from all points of use or otherwise prevented from unintended use.

1978: § 820.181 DEVICE MASTER RECORD

ANSI/ISO/ASQC Q9001-1994

4.5.2 Document and data approval and issue

The documents and data shall be reviewed and approved for adequacy by authorized personnel prior to issue. A master list or equivalent document-control procedure identifying the current revision status of documents shall be established and be readily available to preclude the use of invalid and/or obsolete documents.

This control shall ensure that:

a) the pertinent issues of appropriate documents are available at all locations where operations essential to the effective functioning of the quality system are performed;

b) invalid and/or obsolete documents are promptly removed from all points of issue or use, or otherwise assured against unintended use;

c) any obsolete documents retained for legal and/or knowledge-preservation purposes are suitably identified.

ALSO SEE ISO/DIS 13485:1996, 4.5.2 DOCUMENT AND DATA APPROVAL AND ISSUE

 **FDA GUIDANCE**

§ 820.40 Document controls

§ 820.40(a) Document approval and distribution

The verification of document distribution and removal is very important and can directly affect the quality of a product. Section 820.40, which requires that the manufacturer establish and maintain procedures to control all documents, including those that are obsolete and/or to be removed, requires that the removal (or prevention of use) of obsolete documents be verified. The procedures established must, among other things, ensure control of the accuracy and usage of current versions of the documents and the removal or prevention from use of obsolete documents, as well as ensure that the documentation developed is adequate to fulfill its intended purpose or requirement. The manufacturer must establish a procedure for ensuring that only the current and approved version of a document is used, achieving the objective of the "master list or equivalent document control procedure."

FDA is aware that many documentation systems are now maintained electronically and is in the process of developing an agencywide policy that will be implemented through rulemaking on the use of electronic signatures. The agency identified several important issues related to the use of such signatures, including how to ensure that the identification is in fact the user's "signature." These issues are discussed in FDA's ANPRM on the use of electronic signatures, published in the *Federal*

Register on July 21, 1992 (57 FR 32185), and the proposed regulation published in the *Federal Register* on August 31, 1994 (59 FR 45160). Therefore, FDA notes that the quality system regulation's use of the term "signature" will permit the use of whatever electronic means the agency determines is the equivalent of a handwritten signature. FDA recommends that manufacturers use the two *Federal Register* documents as guidance until the regulation is finalized.

FDA has not added the phrase "or stamps" to the regulation; however, stamps could be acceptable if the manufacturer has a formal procedure on how stamps are used in place of handwritten signatures. The procedure would have to address many of the same issues addressed in the electronic signature *Federal Register* documents, most importantly how the stamps would be controlled and how the manufacturer would ensure that the stamp was in fact the user's "signature."

 **GHTF GUIDANCE**

4.5.2 Document and data approval and issue

The supplier's system should provide a clear and precise control of procedures and responsibilities for approval, issue, distribution, and administration of documentation, including the removal, and possibly preservation, of obsolete documents. This can be accomplished, for example, by maintaining a master list of documents identifying level of approval, distribution (location of copies), and revision status.

Document control should include those documents and/or computer records pertinent to design, purchasing, work execution, quality standards, inspection of materials, and the quality system documents. The supplier's internal written procedures should describe:

—how the documentation for these functions should be controlled;

—who is responsible for the control;

—what is to be controlled;

—where and when the control is to take place.

FDA QUALITY SYSTEM REGULATION—1996

§ 820.40(b) Document changes

Changes to documents shall be reviewed and approved by an individual(s) in the same function or organization that performed the original review and approval, unless specifically designated otherwise.

- Approved changes shall be communicated to the appropriate personnel in a timely manner.
- Each manufacturer shall maintain records of changes to documents. Change records shall include a description of the change, identification of the affected documents, the signature of the approving individual(s), the approval date, and when the change becomes effective.

1978: § 820.181 DEVICE MASTER RECORD

 # ANSI/ISO/ASQC Q9001-1994

4.5.3 Document and data changes

Changes to documents and data shall be reviewed and approved by the same functions/organizations that performed the original review and approval, unless specifically designated otherwise. The designated functions/organizations shall have access to pertinent background information upon which to base their review and approval.

Where practicable, the nature of the change shall be identified in the document or the appropriate attachments.

 # FDA GUIDANCE

§ 820.40(b) Document changes

FDA requires that the approved changes must be communicated in a timely manner to appropriate personnel. FDA has had many experiences where manufacturers made corrections to documents, but the changes were not communicated in a timely manner to the personnel utilizing the documents. The result of these untimely communications was the production of defective devices.

FDA requires that changes be "approved by an individual(s) in the same function or organization that performed the original review and approval, unless specifically designated otherwise." The intent of the requirement is to ensure that those who originally approved the document have an opportunity to review any changes, because these individuals typically have the best insight on the impact of the changes. The requirement is flexible, however, because it permits the manufacturer to specifically designate individuals who did not perform the original review and approval to review and approve the changes. To designate such individuals, the manufacturer will need to determine who would be best suited to perform the function, thus ensuring adequate control over the changes. In this way, review and approval will not be haphazard.

 **GHTF GUIDANCE**

4.5.3 Document and data changes

Recognizing that supplier documentation may be subject to revision and change, controls should exist for the preparation, handling, approval, issue, and recording of changes. These document controls should apply not only to internal documentation but also to documents, such as regulations and standards, which are generated and updated externally but which may form important parts of the design and manufacturing process. The supplier should establish a continuing mechanism for controlling changes in documentation. The mechanism should:

—provide for control irrespective of documentation media;

—follow documented procedures;

—ensure accurate updating of documents;

—provide for using only authorized documents when implementing changes;

—preclude confusion, especially where there is a multiplicity of sources authorizing changes and releasing documents.

Changes that may affect quality should be verified or validated (as appropriate) before implementation.

Consideration should be given to the effect which the proposed changes may have on other parts of the procedure, system, and product (including service). Actions may be needed before a change is implemented to assess the effect of the change on other parts of the organization, and notify them, as appropriate.

Planned circulation of a change proposal to personnel in the affected functions can assist in avoiding disruption. The timing of the implementation of the change may be an important factor, particularly when several changes of documentation are to be coordinated.

Records of an approved change should include a description of the change, the identity of the affected documents, a dated signature, and when the change becomes effective.

The master copy of withdrawn documents should be clearly marked and retained by storage in a secure location. Other copies of withdrawn documents should be disposed of. The object of retaining a single copy of obsolete or superseded documents is to provide a full picture of the product at various stages of its life, from first design considerations through development to present status. It may be possible to achieve this objective by maintaining detailed records of changes as they are made, rather than retaining copies of each issue of every document.

NOTES

NOTES

NOTES

SUBPART E

Purchasing Controls

FDA QUALITY SYSTEM REGULATION—1996

§ 820.50 Purchasing controls

Each manufacturer shall establish and maintain procedures to ensure that all purchased or otherwise received product and services conform to specified requirements.

ANSI/ISO/ASQC Q9001-1994

4.6 Purchasing

4.6.1 General

The supplier shall establish and maintain documented procedures to ensure that purchased product (see 3.1) conforms to specified requirements.

GHTF GUIDANCE

4.6 Purchasing

4.6.1 General

A supplier may purchase, from a number of sources, products and services which may include:

—raw materials;

—components or subassemblies manufactured by others using equipment owned by, and/or materials provided by, the supplier;

—components or subassemblies available as standard items from other sources;

—components or subassemblies manufactured by others to the supplier's specifications;

—completed product bearing the mark and/or name of the supplier; this may be ready for sale or require some further processing such as packaging and/or sterilization;

—services, e.g., sterilization, calibration, testing, pest control, waste disposal, cleaning, environmental monitoring, laundry, transport, installation.

The term "subcontractor" is taken to include all providers of materials, components, subassemblies, finished product, or services.

A distinction may be made between purchase of materials or services to the supplier's specification and the purchase of standard, commercially available materials. This can be useful in deciding on the type and extent of control to be applied to purchased materials or services.

To ensure that purchased, subcontracted products (including services) conform to specified purchaser requirements as well as regulatory requirements, purchasing should be planned and carried out by the supplier under adequate control. This should include the following:

—evaluation and selection of subcontractors (see 4.6.2);

—clear and unambiguous specification of the purchaser requirements (see 4.6.3);

—the performance of suitable verification (see 4.6.4);

—inspection procedures (see 4.10.1).

The supplier should establish an effective working relationship and feedback system with the subcontractor.

 FDA QUALITY SYSTEM REGULATION—1996

§ 820.50(a) Evaluation of suppliers, contractors, and consultants

Each manufacturer shall establish and maintain the requirements, including quality requirements, that must be met by suppliers, contractors, and consultants. Each manufacturer shall:

(1) Evaluate and select potential suppliers, contractors, and consultants on the basis of their ability to meet specified requirements, including quality requirements. The evaluation shall be documented.

(2) Define the type and extent of control to be exercised over the product, services, suppliers, contractors, and consultants, based on the evaluation results.

(3) Establish and maintain records of acceptable suppliers, contractors, and consultants.

1978: § 820.81(a) ACCEPTANCE OF CRITICAL COMPONENTS

ANSI/ISO/ASQC Q9001-1994

4.6.2 Evaluation of subcontractors

The supplier shall:

a) evaluate and select subcontractors on the basis of their ability to meet subcontract requirements including the quality system and any specific quality-assurance requirements;

b) define the type and extent of control exercised by the supplier over subcontractors. This shall be dependent upon the type of product, the impact of subcontracted product on the quality of final product, and, where applicable, on the quality audit reports and/or quality records of the previously demonstrated capability and performance of subcontractors;

c) establish and maintain quality records of acceptable subcontractors (see 4.16).

FDA GUIDANCE

§ 820.50 Purchasing controls

§ 820.50(a) Evaluation of suppliers, contractors, and consultants

The failure to implement adequate purchasing controls has resulted in a significant number of recalls due to component failures. Most of these were due to unacceptable components provided by suppliers. Since FDA is not regulating component suppliers, it

believes that the explicit addition to CGMP requirements of the purchasing controls of ISO 9001:1994 is necessary to provide the additional assurance that only acceptable components are used. To ensure that purchased or otherwise received product or services conform to specifications, purchasing must be carried out under adequate controls, including the assessment and selection of suppliers, contractors, and consultants; the clear and unambiguous specification of requirements; and the performance of suitable acceptance activities. Each manufacturer must establish an appropriate mix of assessment and receiving acceptance to ensure that products and services are acceptable for their intended uses. The specifications for the finished device cannot be met unless the individual parts of the finished device meet specifications. The most efficient and least costly approach is to ensure that only acceptable products and services are received. This means that only suppliers, contractors, and consultants that meet specifications should be used.

The regulation has been written to allow flexibility in the way manufacturers may ensure the acceptability of products and services. Under the requirements, manufacturers must clearly define in the procedures the type and extent of control they intend to apply to products and services. Thus, a finished device manufacturer may choose to provide greater in-house controls to ensure that products and services meet requirements, or may require the supplier to adopt measures necessary to ensure acceptability, as appropriate. FDA generally believes that an appropriate mix of supplier and manufacturer quality controls are necessary. However, finished device manufacturers who conduct product quality control solely in-house must also assess the capability of suppliers to provide acceptable product. Where audits are not practical, this may be done through, among other means, reviewing historical data, monitoring and trending, and inspection and testing.

Thus the degree of supplier control necessary to establish compliance may vary with the type and significance of the product or service purchased and the impact of that product or service on the quality of the finished device. The requirement for manufacturers to establish assessment criteria is not explicitly stated, but the evaluation still must include a description of how the assessment was made (according to what criteria or objective procedure) and the results must be documented. Each manufacturer must define the type and extent of control it will exercise over suppliers, contractors, and consultants. Suppliers, contractors, and consultants selected by manufacturers of medical devices should have a demonstrated capability of providing products and services that meet the requirements established by the finished device manufacturer. The capability of the product or service suppliers should be reviewed at intervals consistent with the significance of the product or service provided, and the review should demonstrate conformance to specified requirements.

FDA emphasizes that the requirements apply to all product and service received from outside of the finished device manufacturer, whether payment occurs or not. Thus, a manufacturer must comply with these provisions when it receives product or services from its "sister facility" or some other corporate or financial affiliate.

Each manufacturer must establish procedures to ensure that received product and services (purchased or otherwise received) conform to specified requirements. All manufacturers are expected to apply controls to manufacturing materials appropriate to the manufacturing material, the intended use, and the effect of the manufacturing materials on safety and effectiveness. For example, the procedures necessary to ensure that a mold release agent conforms to specified requirements may be less involved than the procedures for controlling latex proteins. The provision allows the manufacturer the flexibility of establishing the procedures to meet its needs and to ensure that the product conforms to specified requirements.

 **GHTF GUIDANCE**

4.6.2 Evaluation of subcontractors

The supplier may employ several ways of choosing satisfactory subcontractors, given that technical capabilities are satisfactory for the product to be delivered, for example:

—a review of previous performance in supplying similar products, processes, or services;

—a satisfactory evaluation to an appropriate quality system standard by a body considered to be competent for the purpose;

—an evaluation of the subcontractor by the supplier to an appropriate quality system standard.

The supplier's quality records concerning the evaluation should be sufficiently comprehensive to demonstrate the ability of subcontractors to meet contract requirements and should allow for selection on the basis of quality capability.

Factors such as product compliance with specified requirements, the total cost for the supplier, delivery arrangements, and the subcontractor's own quality systems may be pertinent in this context. The performance of subcontractors should be reviewed at intervals consistent with the complexity and technical requirements of the product and demonstrated subcontractor performance.

 FDA QUALITY SYSTEM REGULATION—1996

§ 820.50(b) Purchasing data

Each manufacturer shall establish and maintain data that clearly describe or reference the specified requirements, including quality requirements, for purchased or otherwise received product and services.

- Purchasing documents shall include, where possible, an agreement that the suppliers, contractors, and consultants agree to notify the manufacturer of changes in the product or service so that manufacturers may determine whether the change may affect the quality of a finished device.
- Purchasing data shall be approved in accordance with § 820.40.

1978: § 820.81(b) CRITICAL COMPONENT SUPPLIER AGREEMENT

 **ANSI/ISO/ASQC Q9001-1994**

4.6.3 Purchasing data

Purchasing documents shall contain data clearly describing the product ordered, including where applicable:

a) the type, class, grade, or other precise identification;

b) the title or other positive identification, and applicable issues of specifications, drawings, process requirements, inspection instructions, and other relevant technical data, including requirements for approval or qualification of product, procedures, process equipment, and personnel;

c) the title, number, and issue of the quality-system standard to be applied.

The supplier shall review and approve purchasing documents for adequacy of the specified requirements prior to release.

ALSO SEE ISO/DIS 13485:1996, 4.6.3 PURCHASING DATA

 **FDA GUIDANCE**

§ 820.50(b) Purchasing data

This requirement is for approval of purchasing data or information on the purchasing document used to purchase a product or service. Thus, each manufacturer must review and approve the purchasing data before release of the data. FDA believes that supplier change information is very important to the manufacturer and that the manufacturer should obtain information on changes to the product or service. Where a supplier refuses to agree to provide such notification, depending on the product or service being purchased, it may render that company an unacceptable supplier. Where the product is in short supply and must be purchased, however, the manufacturer will need to heighten control in other ways.

Specifications for many manufacturing materials may be so well established that the trade name of the product may be sufficient to describe the material needed. For other materials, specific written specifications may be necessary to ensure that the desired materials are received. The extent of the specification detail necessary to ensure that the product or service purchased meets requirements will be related to the nature of the product or service purchased, taking into account the effect the product or service may have on the safety or effectiveness of the finished device, among other factors.

 **GHTF GUIDANCE**

4.6.3 Purchasing data

Clarity in the specification documents and the subcontractor's agreement that the product or service can be supplied in accordance with the specification are essential ingredients of success in subcontracting. The subcontract should also include an agreement between both parties on the methods of quality assurance that will be used to decide the acceptability of product or service.

The supplier's purchasing data should define the specified technical product requirements to the subcontractor to ensure the quality of the purchased product, process, service. This may be done, in part, by reference to other applicable technical information such as national or international standards, test methods, etc. Well-defined purchase orders can provide documented evidence. Another option is for essential information to be clearly and precisely stated in the subcontract. Responsibilities for reviewing and approving the purchasing data should be clearly assigned to appropriate personnel. Arrangements should be made to identify the revision status of documents referenced in the purchasing data.

Where justified by the use of the device, the purchasing agreement should include a requirement for the subcontractor to give advance notice to the supplier of any changes (e.g., of materials) that could affect the quality of the product or service supplied.

NOTES

NOTES

F
Identification and Traceability

FDA QUALITY SYSTEM REGULATION—1996

§ 820.60 Identification

Each manufacturer shall establish and maintain procedures for identifying product during all stages of receipt, production, distribution, and installation to prevent mixups.

1978: § 820.80 COMPONENTS

FDA GUIDANCE

§ 820.60 Identification

Section 820.60 is broad enough to allow the manufacturer the flexibility needed to identify product by whatever means described by the required procedure. The purpose of this requirement is to ensure that all products, including manufacturing materials used in the manufacture of a finished device, are properly identified. This requirement is intended to help prevent inadvertent use or release of unacceptable product into manufacturing. It is as important that the proper manufacturing materials be used as it is that the proper component be used.

Section 820.60 only requires that product be identified but says nothing about the acceptance status of that product. Section 820.86 requires that the acceptance status be identified so that inadvertent use of product does not occur. The manufacturer may choose to set up a system by which the identification required by § 820.60 can also show the acceptance status required by § 820.86, but this is up to the manufacturer.

FDA QUALITY SYSTEM REGULATION—1996

§ 820.65 Traceability

Each manufacturer of a device that is intended for surgical implant into the body or to support or sustain life and whose failure to perform when properly used in accordance with instructions for use provided in the labeling can be reasonably expected to result in a significant injury to the user shall establish and maintain procedures for identifying with a control number each unit, lot, or batch of finished devices and where appropriate components.

- The procedures shall facilitate corrective action.
- Such identification shall be documented in the device history record.

1978: § 820.151 CRITICAL DEVICE, DISTRIBUTION RECORDS

 # ANSI/ISO/ASQC Q9001-1994

4.8 Product identification and traceability

Where appropriate, the supplier shall establish and maintain documented procedures for identifying the product by suitable means from receipt and during all stages of production, delivery, and installation.

Where and to the extent that traceability is a specified requirement, the supplier shall establish and maintain documented procedures for unique identification of individual product or batches. This identification shall be recorded (see 4.16).

ALSO SEE ISO/DIS 13485:1996, 4.8 PRODUCT IDENTIFICATION AND TRACEABILITY

 # FDA GUIDANCE

§ 820.65 Traceability

Section 820.65 uses the definition of a "critical device" from the original CGMP to provide the necessary clarity and delineation for this requirement. Thus, traceability is required for the critical devices listed in the *Federal Register* notice of March 17, 1988 (53 FR 8854). FDA is using the definition of critical device in the requirement of § 820.65, however, rather than a reference to the 1988 list of critical devices, because that list has not been updated since 1988 and there are no plans to revise that list. Therefore, it is imperative that manufacturers use the definition within the requirement of § 820.65 to determine if a particular device needs to be traced; it may not be sufficient to rely solely on the 1988 list.

It is important that the traceability requirements in part 820 are not confused with the medical device tracking regulation in part 821 (21 CFR part 821). The tracking regulation is intended to ensure that tracked devices can be traced from the device manufacturing facility to the person for whom the device is indicated, that is, the patient. Effective tracking of devices from the manufacturing facility, through the distribution network (including distributors, retailers, rental firms and other commercial enterprises, device user facilities, and licensed practitioners) and, ultimately, to any person for whom the device is intended, is necessary for the effectiveness of remedies prescribed by the act, such as patient notification (section 518(a) of the act (21 U.S.C. 360h(a)) or device recall (section 518(e)). In contrast, the traceability provision requires that a device that meets the definition of a "critical device" can be traced from the manufacturing facility only to the "initial consignee," as discussed in § 820.160, "Distribution."

Manufacturers may find it advantageous to provide unit, lot, or batch traceability for devices for which traceability is not a requirement to facilitate control and limit the number of devices that may need to be recalled due to defects or violations of the act. The requirement also mandates traceability of components "where appropriate," limited by the discussion in the scope, § 820.1(a)(3). The critical component definition in the original CGMP regulation may be used as guidance. To carry out the requirement, however, the manufacturer should perform risk analysis first on the finished device, and subsequently on the components of such a device, to determine the need for traceability. FDA believes that the extent of traceability for both active and inactive implantable devices should include all components and materials used when such products could cause the medical device not to satisfy its specified requirements. ISO/CD 13485 also requires that the manufacturer's agents or distributors maintain records of distribution of medical devices with regard to traceability and that such records be available for inspection. This requirement is found in § 820.160, "Distribution," of this regulation and is consistent with the requirements in § 820.151 of the original CGMP.

While FDA understands that traceability entails additional cost, the agency notes that if a product recall is necessary, more devices would be subject to recall if units, lots, or batches of specific devices are not traceable, with associated higher recall costs to the manufacturer.

 **GHTF GUIDANCE**

4.8 Product identification and traceability

The supplier can achieve product identification by marking or tagging the product or its container. For example, on visually identical parts where the functional characteristics are different, different colors can be used. For bulk products or product from continuous processes, the identification may be limited to identification of batches or well-defined lots.

Service identification can be achieved by documentation that accompanies the service. Product (including service) traceability involves the ability to trace the history, application, or location of an item or activity by means of recorded identification. Traceability can entail high cost, and the extent of this requirement should be carefully considered. The traceability requirement of the destination country should always be considered when establishing traceability procedures.

The supplier can achieve traceability by each individual product having an identifier (e.g., serial number, date code, batch code, lot number) unique to the source of operation. Separate identifiers could be required for changes in operative personnel, changes in raw materials, changes in tooling, new or different machine setups, changes in process methods, etc. Traceability identifiers should appear on applicable inspection and stock records. For example, adequate traceability can avoid the unnecessary explant of implantable medical devices through precise identification of those implants which incorporate a subsequently identified faulty component, or for which some process control has subsequently been shown to be inadequate. This implies continuing the traceability up to the point of implantation, although this may not always be within the capability of the supplier. Traceability records should be maintained throughout the lifetime of the product.

NOTES

NOTES

Production and Process Controls

 FDA QUALITY SYSTEM REGULATION—1996

§ 820.70 Production and process controls

§ 820.70(a) *General.* Each manufacturer shall develop, conduct, control, and monitor production processes to ensure that a device conforms to its specifications.

- Where deviations from device specifications could occur as a result of the manufacturing process, the manufacturer shall establish and maintain process control procedures that describe any process controls necessary to ensure conformance to specifications.

- Where process controls are needed they shall include:
  (1) Documented instructions, standard operating procedures (SOPs), and methods that define and control the manner of production;

  (2) Monitoring and control of process parameters and component and device characteristics during production;

  (3) Compliance with specified reference standards or codes;

  (4) The approval of processes and process equipment; and

  (5) Criteria for workmanship which shall be expressed in documented standards or by means of identified and approved representative samples.

1978: § 820.100 MANUFACTURING SPECIFICATIONS AND PROCESSES AND § 820.100(b)(1 & 2) PROCESSING CONTROLS

FDA GUIDANCE

§ 820.70 Production and process controls

The requirements in § 820.70(a) are intended to ensure that each manufacturer produces devices that conform to their specifications. Thus, where any deviations from specifications could occur during manufacturing, the process control procedures must describe those controls necessary to ensure conformance. Those controls listed in the regulation may not always be relevant; similarly, others may be necessary. For example, where deviations from device specifications could occur as a result of the absence of written production methods, procedures, and workmanship criteria, such production controls are required.

The procedures may be tailored under the requirement to cover only those controls necessary to ensure that a device meets its specifications. The general requirement also serves to tie the production and process controls to the design and development phase where many of these controls are originally established in order for the device to conform to its design specifications.

FDA QUALITY SYSTEM REGULATION—1996

§ 820.70(b) Production and process changes

Each manufacturer shall establish and maintain procedures for changes to a specification, method, process, or procedure.

- Such changes shall be verified or where appropriate validated according to § 820.75, before implementation and these activities shall be documented.
- Changes shall be approved in accordance with § 820.40.

1978: § 820.100(b)(3) PROCESSING CONTROLS

FDA GUIDANCE

§ 820.70(b) Production and process changes

This section addresses the requirement for production and process changes to be "verified or where appropriate validated according to § 820.75." Verification was added to give the manufacturer the flexibility to verify changes that can be tested and inspected because FDA believes that validation is not always necessary. The agency notes that wherever changes may influence a validated process, the process must be revalidated as described in § 820.75. A few examples of processes that must be validated include sterilization, molding, and welding.

 FDA QUALITY SYSTEM REGULATION—1996

§ 820.70(c) Environmental control

Where environmental conditions could reasonably be expected to have an adverse effect on product quality, the manufacturer shall establish and maintain procedures to adequately control these environmental conditions.

*   Environmental control system(s) shall be periodically inspected to verify that the system, including necessary equipment, is adequate and functioning properly.
*   These activities shall be documented and reviewed.

1978: § 820.46 ENVIRONMENTAL CONTROL

 **FDA GUIDANCE**

§ 820.70(c) Environmental control

Section 820.70(c) applies only where environmental conditions could "reasonably be expected to have an adverse effect on product quality." Lighting, ventilation, temperature, humidity, air pressure, filtration, airborne contamination, and static electricity are among many conditions that should be considered for control.

 FDA QUALITY SYSTEM REGULATION—1996

§ 820.70(d) Personnel

Each manufacturer shall establish and maintain requirements for the health, cleanliness, personal practices, and clothing of personnel if contact between such personnel and product or environment could reasonably be expected to have an adverse effect on product quality. The manufacturer shall ensure that maintenance and other personnel who are required to work temporarily under special environmental conditions are appropriately trained or supervised by a trained individual.

1978: § 820.25(b) PERSONNEL HEALTH AND CLEANLINESS, § 820.56(a) PERSONNEL SANITATION, AND § 820.56(c) PERSONNEL PRACTICES

FDA GUIDANCE

§ 820.70(d) Personnel

Under this section, a manufacturer's requirements must not permit unclean or inappropriately clothed employees, or employees with certain medical conditions, to work with devices where such conditions could reasonably be expected to have an adverse effect on product quality. The procedures must also address acceptable clothing, hygiene, and personal practices, if contact between personnel and product or environment could reasonably be expected to have an adverse effect on product quality.

FDA also added the requirement, from ISO/CD 13485, that personnel who are working temporarily (such as maintenance and cleaning personnel) under special environmental conditions (such as a clean room) be appropriately trained or supervised by someone trained to work in such an environment.

FDA QUALITY SYSTEM REGULATION—1996

§ 820.70(e) Contamination control

Each manufacturer shall establish and maintain procedures to prevent contamination of equipment or product by substances that could reasonably be expected to have an adverse effect on product quality.

1978: § 820.56(b) CONTAMINATION CONTROL AND § 820.56(d) SEWAGE AND REFUSE DISPOSAL

§ 820.70(e) Contamination control

This section contains a broad requirement for the establishment of procedures to prevent contamination of equipment or product by any substance that could reasonably be expected to have an adverse effect on product quality. Sewage, trash, byproducts, chemical effluvium, and other refuse that could affect a device's safety, effectiveness, or fitness-for-use must be adequately controlled.

 **FDA QUALITY SYSTEM REGULATION—1996**

§ 820.70(f) Buildings

Buildings shall be of suitable design and contain sufficient space to perform necessary operations, prevent mixups, and assure orderly handling.

1978: § 820.40 BUILDINGS

 **FDA GUIDANCE**

§ 820.70(f) Buildings

The sufficiency of facilities is covered in this section and requires that buildings be of suitable design and contain sufficient space to allow for the proper manufacture of devices. Section 820.70(f) is worded similarly to the original CGMP regulation § 820.40 and is intended to achieve the same objectives as that section.

FDA QUALITY SYSTEM REGULATION—1996

§ 820.70(g) Equipment

Each manufacturer shall ensure that all equipment used in the manufacturing process meets specified requirements and is appropriately designed, constructed, placed, and installed to facilitate maintenance, adjustment, cleaning, and use.

(1) *Maintenance schedule.* Each manufacturer shall establish and maintain schedules for the adjustment, cleaning, and other maintenance of equipment to ensure that manufacturing specifications are met. Maintenance activities, including the date and individual(s) performing the maintenance activities, shall be documented.

(2) *Inspection.* Each manufacturer shall conduct periodic inspections in accordance with established procedures to ensure adherence to applicable equipment maintenance schedules. The inspections, including the date and individual(s) conducting the inspections, shall be documented.

(3) *Adjustment.* Each manufacturer shall ensure that any inherent limitations or allowable tolerances are visibly posted on or near equipment requiring periodic adjustments or are readily available to personnel performing these adjustments.

1978: § 820.60 EQUIPMENT, § 820.60(a) MAINTENANCE SCHEDULE, § 820.60(b) INSPECTION, AND § 820.56(c) ADJUSTMENT

 **FDA GUIDANCE**

§ 820.70(g) Equipment

Equipment must be appropriately designed to facilitate maintenance, adjustment, cleaning, and use. It must also meet the requirements that are necessary to ensure its proper functioning for the manufacture of the device. This section directs a manufacturer to ensure that equipment meets specified requirements and requires that the manufacturer ensure that maintenance is carried out on schedule to comply with the requirement. To satisfactorily meet this requirement, FDA expects that the schedule will be posted on or near the equipment to be maintained, or otherwise be made readily available to appropriate personnel. Also, inherent limitations and allowable tolerances must be visibly posted on or near equipment, or made readily available to personnel to allow the manufacturer the flexibility to utilize any system to make sure that the limitations or tolerances are readily available to the personnel that need them.

FDA QUALITY SYSTEM REGULATION—1996

§ 820.70(h) Manufacturing material

Where a manufacturing material could reasonably be expected to have an adverse effect on product quality, the manufacturer shall establish and maintain procedures for the use and removal of such manufacturing material to ensure that it is removed or limited to an amount that does not adversely affect the device's quality. The removal or reduction of such manufacturing material shall be documented.

1978: § 820.60(d) MANUFACTURING MATERIAL

 ## FDA GUIDANCE

§ 820.70(h) Manufacturing material

This section requires that "where a manufacturing material could reasonably be expected to have an adverse effect on product quality," the manufacturing material shall be removed or reduced and this process documented. FDA purposefully qualifies the general requirement by that which adversely affects "product quality" (product as defined in § 820.3(r)) and limits the requirement for removal or reduction to "an amount that does not adversely affect the device's quality."

 ## FDA QUALITY SYSTEM REGULATION—1996

§ 820.70(i) Automated processes

When computers or automated data processing systems are used as part of production or the quality system, the manufacturer shall validate computer software for its intended use according to an established protocol.

- All software changes shall be validated before approval and issuance.
- These validation activities and results shall be documented.

1978: § 820.61 MEASUREMENT EQUIPMENT AND § 820.195 CRITICAL DEVICES, AUTOMATED DATA PROCESSING

 **FDA GUIDANCE**

§ 820.70(i) Automated processes

FDA has maintained the requirement for validation of computers or automated data processing systems that are part of production or the quality system because the agency believes that it is necessary that software be validated to the extent possible to adequately ensure performance. Where source code and design specifications cannot be obtained, "black box testing" must be performed to confirm that the software meets the user's needs and its intended uses. FDA emphasizes that manufacturers are responsible for the adequacy of the software used in their devices and activities used to produce devices. When manufacturers purchase off-the-shelf software, they must ensure that it will perform as intended in its chosen application. Software used in production or the quality system, whether it be in the designing, manufacturing, distributing, or tracing, must be validated.

 ANSI/ISO/ASQC Q9001-1994

4.9 Process control

The supplier shall identify and plan the production, installation, and servicing processes which directly affect quality and shall ensure that these processes are carried out under controlled conditions. Controlled conditions shall include the following:

a)   documented procedures defining the manner of production, installation, and servicing, where the absence of such procedures could adversely affect quality;

b)   use of suitable production, installation, and servicing equipment, and a suitable working environment;

c)   compliance with reference standards/codes, quality plans, and/or documented procedures;

d)   monitoring and control of suitable process parameters and product characteristics;

e)   the approval of processes and equipment, as appropriate;

f)   criteria for workmanship, which shall be stipulated in the clearest practical manner (e.g., written standards, representative samples, or illustrations);

g)   suitable maintenance of equipment to ensure continuing process capability.

Where the results of processes cannot be fully verified by subsequent inspection and testing of the product and where, for example, processing deficiencies may become apparent only after the product is in use, the processes shall be carried out by qualified operators and/or shall require continuous monitoring and control of process parameters to ensure that the specified requirements are met.

The requirements for any qualification of process operations, including associated equipment and personnel (see 4.18), shall be specified.

NOTE 16 Such processes requiring prequalification of their process capability are frequently referred to as special processes.

Records shall be maintained for qualified processes, equipment, and personnel, as appropriate (see 4.16).

ALSO SEE ISO/DIS 13485:1996, 4.9 PROCESS CONTROL

 **GHTF GUIDANCE**

4.9 Process control

The supplier's planning for the production and, where applicable, installation processes should consider each of the controlled conditions described in ISO 9001. Control within the process to prevent nonconformities from occurring is preferable to inspection of finished product or service alone. The characteristics which are most critical to the product/service quality should be identified and should be under the closest process control.

Both written and electronic media documentation methods should be recognized for documented procedures.

Process-control activities may include procedures for accepting materials or items into the process and determining their characteristics while in the process. The amount of testing and inspecting needed for process control may bear a relationship to the influence of nonconformities on the downstream process. The adequacy of measurement processes should be considered in assessing the adequacy of production process control.

Where suitable, process control should include statistical process-control methods, supplemented by procedures to maintain the suitability of software, of in-process materials, and of activities needed for appropriate storage, handling, and segregation.

PRODUCTION AND PROCESS CONTROLS

Where the achievement of desired levels of process control is dependent upon consistent and stable operation of process equipment and essential materials, the supplier should include within the scope of the quality system the proper maintenance of such process equipment and essential materials.

Before and during the introduction of a new or significantly changed product (see also 4.4 of this guidance), the manufacturing process, including any new manufacturing and test methods, should be fully evaluated. The key variables and acceptance limits should be identified and validated for processes, test methods, and sampling plans. Similar procedures should be followed where any significant change in processing occurs. The results of validation exercises should be documented. Processes should be reexamined at appropriate intervals to ensure that they are operating within the validated acceptance limits.

WORK IN PROGRESS

Work-in-progress should be identified and/or segregated to avoid product mixup and to ensure traceability where necessary (see 4.8 of this guidance). For small parts, for bulk manufacture, and where the parts cannot be marked, the bulk containers and/or process equipment may be identified to indicate the product and/or batch. This identification need not be the code used on the finished product, but it should be easily related to this code. Any previously used labels should be removed or obliterated.

Ancillary materials should be adequately identified and labeled. Containers for temporary storage and handling should be suitably constructed and cleaned as necessary.

EQUIPMENT

Where automated production or quality control systems are used, any software and/or hardware should be validated. Software and changes to software may be controlled in the same manner as documents, i.e., program authorized on issue, master copy of the original program retained, control and validation of changes to programs with revision levels, and retention of superseded copies (see also section 4.5 of this guidance). ISO 9000-3 may be used as a reference in the control of software.

MAINTENANCE OF EQUIPMENT

Documented procedures should be available for the maintenance and checking of all equipment used in production and for environmental control. The determination of the necessary adjustments and maintenance intervals should be established during the commissioning and validation of new equipment.

PREMISES

The design, construction, and maintenance of premises can influence product quality. Buildings in which manufacture, assembly, packaging, storage, inspection and test, and labeling are carried out should be of suitable design and contain sufficient space to facilitate cleaning, maintenance, and other necessary operations.

The following are examples of features to be considered in the design and construction of premises: lighting, temperature, humidity, ventilation, air pressure, filtration, airborne particulate contamination, microbial contamination, and possibility of electrostatic discharge. Special handling procedures may be required to protect circuit components from damage due to electrostatic discharges.

Features which can affect the quality of product may include: cleanliness, environmental conditions, segregation of materials, access for personnel, storage facilities, waste disposal arrangements, and provision for eating, drinking, and smoking areas. Some of the provisions that should be considered where they may affect product quality are:

—flow of material through manufacturing;

—access for personnel;

—cloakroom and toilet facilities, segregated from production areas;

—maintenance, repair, building activities; the desirability of documenting maintenance activities;

—pest control; the avoidance of product contamination by pest control materials;

—gas, electricity, water, etc.;

—special manufacturing operations;

—the segregation of "dirty," or dust-generating, activities from "clean" processes or areas;

—disposal of waste material;

—special storage areas and conditions;

—special testing and laboratory facilities.

CLEANING OF PREMISES AND EQUIPMENT

Documented cleaning procedures for all general areas and equipment may include:

—cleaning equipment and materials to be used;

—methods to be used;

—methods of protection of products from contamination during cleaning;

—frequency of cleaning;

—designated personnel;

—records to be kept;

—instructions for periodic major cleaning;

—storage of cleaning equipment in a clean, dry, and tidy manner.

When cleaning operations are carried out by a subcontractor, there should be a written contract specifying the limits of responsibility of both parties. This contract should include details of the documented cleaning procedure and specify the training to be given to cleaning staff (see also 4.18 of this guidance).

INSTALLATION

If a medical device has to be assembled or installed at the user's site, instructions should be provided by the supplier to guide correct assembly, installation, and/or calibration, which is the final stage of manufacture. Special attention should be paid to correct installation of safety control mechanisms and safety control circuits.

In certain cases, for example when required by regulation, where performance parameters of a medical device have to be controlled, the supplier should provide instructions that allow the installer to confirm correct operation of the device. The results of installation or commissioning tests should be documented.

SPECIAL PROCESSES

The supplier should give special consideration to "special processes." These are processes in which the product quality characteristics cannot fully be verified in the finished product. Examples include circumstances where:

—the characteristics of interest do not exist until further downstream in the process;

—the method of measurement does not exist or is destructive to the product;

—results within the process cannot be measured in later inspections or tests.

All products are produced by processes, and "special processes" are found in all generic product categories: hardware, software, processed materials, and services. However, "special processes" are particularly common in producing processed materials.

Some examples where critical product quality characteristics fall within one or more of the three process circumstances above include:

—strength, ductility, fatigue life, corrosion resistance of a metal part following welding, soldering, heat treatment, or plating;

—dyeability, shrinkage, tensile properties of a polymer;

—correct implementation of a software product, or cleanliness/sterility of a medical device.

Such products are typically the final result of a series of operations and require close adherence to specified in-process procedures and sequences. For a processed material or hardware product these can involve starting materials, temperature profiles, physical deformations, mixing, and environmental conditions. For a software or service product these can involve source data and documents, intellectual, and clerical correctness.

Comprehensive measurement assurance and calibration of equipment used to produce or measure the product may be required for such "special processes." The use of statistical process control is often most advantageous.

Special skills, capabilities, and training of personnel may be needed and should be demonstrated.

Process knowledge can be considered as a basis to distinguish finished-product characteristics from measurable in-process characteristics. Such processes should be validated in advance to ensure that the process will meet the specified requirements.

 # FDA QUALITY SYSTEM REGULATION—1996

§ 820.72 Inspection, measuring, and test equipment

§ 820.72(a) Control of inspection, measuring, and test equipment

Each manufacturer shall ensure that all inspection, measuring, and test equipment, including mechanical, automated, or electronic inspection and test equipment, is suitable for its intended purposes and is capable of producing valid results.

- Each manufacturer shall establish and maintain procedures to ensure that equipment is routinely calibrated, inspected, checked, and maintained.

- The procedures shall include provisions for handling, preservation, and storage of equipment, so that its accuracy and fitness for use are maintained.

- These activities shall be documented.

1978: § 820.61 MEASUREMENT EQUIPMENT

§ 820.72(b) Calibration

Calibration procedures shall include specific directions and limits for accuracy and precision. When accuracy and precision limits are not met, there shall be provisions for remedial action to reestablish the limits and to evaluate whether there was any adverse effect on the device's quality. These activities shall be documented.

(1) *Calibration standards.* Calibration standards used for inspection, measuring, and test equipment shall be traceable to national or international standards.

- If national or international standards are not practical or available, the manufacturer shall use an independent reproducible standard.

- If no applicable standard exists, the manufacturer shall establish and maintain an in-house standard.

(2) *Calibration records.* The equipment identification, calibration dates, the individual performing each calibration, and the next calibration date shall be documented. These records shall be displayed on or near each piece of equipment or shall be readily available to the personnel using such equipment and to the individuals responsible for calibrating the equipment.

ANSI/ISO/ASQC Q9001-1994

4.11 Control of inspection, measuring, and test equipment

4.11.1 General

The supplier shall establish and maintain documented procedures to control, calibrate, and maintain inspection, measuring, and test equipment (including test software) used by the supplier to demonstrate the conformance of product to the specified requirements. Inspection, measuring, and test equipment shall be used in a manner which ensures that the measurement uncertainty is known and is consistent with the required measurement capability.

Where test software or comparative references such as test hardware are used as suitable forms of inspection, they shall be checked to prove that they are capable of verifying the acceptability of product, prior to release for use during production, installation, or servicing, and shall be rechecked at prescribed intervals. The supplier shall establish the extent and frequency of such checks and shall maintain records as evidence of control (see 4.16).

Where the availability of technical data pertaining to the measurement equipment is a specified requirement, such data shall be made available, when required by the customer or customer's representative, for verification that the measuring equipment is functionally adequate.

NOTE 17 For the purposes of this American National Standard, the term "measuring equipment" includes measurement devices.

4.11.2 Control procedure

The supplier shall:

a)   determine the measurements to be made and the accuracy required, and select the appropriate inspection, measuring, and test equipment that is capable of the necessary accuracy and precision;

b)   identify all inspection, measuring, and test equipment that can affect product quality, and calibrate and adjust them at prescribed intervals, or prior to use, against certified equipment having a known valid relationship to internationally or nationally recognized standards. Where no such standards exist, the basis used for calibration shall be documented;

c)   define the process employed for the calibration of inspection, measuring, and test equipment, including details of equipment type, unique identification, location, frequency of checks, check method, acceptance criteria, and the action to be taken when results are unsatisfactory;

d)   identify inspection, measuring, and test equipment with a suitable indicator or approved identification record to show the calibration status;

e)   maintain calibration records for inspection, measuring, and test equipment (see 4.16);

f)   assess and document the validity of previous inspection and test results when inspection, measuring, and test equipment is found to be out of calibration;

g)   ensure that the environmental conditions are suitable for the calibrations, inspections, measurements, and tests being carried out;

h)   ensure that the handling, preservation, and storage of inspection, measuring, and test equipment is such that the accuracy and fitness for use are maintained;

i)   safeguard inspection, measuring, and test facilities, including both test hardware and test software, from adjustments which would invalidate the calibration setting.

NOTE 18 The metrological confirmation system for measuring equipment given in ISO 10012 may be used for guidance.

 **FDA GUIDANCE**

§ 820.72 Inspection, measuring, and test equipment

FDA has added to this section the requirement that the calibration procedure include provisions for remedial action to "reestablish the limits and to evaluate whether there was any adverse effect on the device's quality" to clarify this requirement and its relationship to the requirements in § 820.100, "Corrective and preventive action."

This section also includes a requirement for maintenance procedures for inspection, measuring, and test equipment because some equipment requires special handling, preservation, and storage. For example, the temperature and humidity of a room may affect the equipment, and procedures would need to be established taking those factors into account. The procedures must also ensure that equipment is protected from adjustments that could invalidate the calibration. The procedures that require equipment to be routinely calibrated, inspected, and checked will also ensure that improperly calibrated equipment is not used.

 GHTF GUIDANCE

4.11 Control of inspection, measuring, and test equipment

4.11.1 General

4.11.2 Control procedure

The requirements of this clause in ISO 9001 spell out in considerable detail what is to be implemented. Although the requirements pertain explicitly to inspection, measuring, and test equipment, it is helpful to approach the subject from the perspective that measuring is itself a process involving raw materials, equipment, and procedures. The requirements of ISO 9001 explicitly involve elements of the measurement process; elements whose collective purpose is to choose suitable measurements, suitable measuring equipment, and suitable measurement procedures. These elements are specified to provide confidence in the ability of the supplier's measuring systems to control adequately the production and inspection of the product.

For both product- and process-measurement systems, statistical methods are valuable tools for achieving and demonstrating fulfillment of requirements. In particular, statistical methods are the preferred tools in fulfilling the requirement that "inspection, measuring and test equipment shall be used in a manner which ensures that the measurement uncertainty is known and is consistent with the required measurement capability."

The requirements of this clause also should be applied by the supplier insofar as "demonstrating the conformance of product to the specified requirements" contractually involves measurements subsequent to production and inspection of a product (e.g., during subsequent handling, storage, packaging, delivery, or servicing) as may be required under other clauses of ISO 9001.

§ 820.75 Process validation

§ 820.75(a). Where the results of a process cannot be fully verified by subsequent inspection and test, the process shall be validated with a high degree of assurance and approved according to established procedures. The validation activities and results, including the date and signature of the individual(s) approving the validation and where appropriate the major equipment validated, shall be documented.

1978: § 820.100(a)(1) SPECIFICATION CONTROLS

§ 820.75(b). Each manufacturer shall establish and maintain procedures for monitoring and control of process parameters for validated processes to ensure that the specified requirements continue to be met.

(1) Each manufacturer shall ensure that validated processes are performed by qualified individual(s).

(2) For validated processes, the monitoring and control methods and data, the date performed, and, where appropriate, the individual(s) performing the process or the major equipment used shall be documented.

1978: § 820.100(b)(1 & 2) PROCESSING CONTROLS AND § 820.101 CRITICAL DEVICES, MANUFACTURING SPECIFICATIONS AND PROCESSES

§ 820.75(c). When changes or process deviations occur, the manufacturer shall review and evaluate the process and perform revalidation where appropriate. These activities shall be documented.

1978: § 820.100(b)(3) PROCESSING CONTROLS

SEE ALSO ANSI/ISO/ASQC Q9001-1994, 4.9 PROCESS CONTROL

 # FDA GUIDANCE

§ 820.75 Process validation

This section requires that when a process "cannot be fully verified by subsequent inspection and test, the process shall be validated with a high degree of assurance." Examples of such processes include sterilization, aseptic processing, injection molding, and welding. The validation method must ensure that predetermined specifications are consistently met.

Depending on the process that is validated, it may be necessary to document the person performing the process or the equipment or both in order to have adequate controls on the process. FDA emphasizes that validated processes must not only be performed by personnel with the necessary education, background, training, and experience for their general jobs, but must be performed by personnel qualified for those particular functions. FDA notes that it is always "appropriate" to document the equipment used in the process where the manufacturer uses different equipment on different manufacturing lines. To investigate a problem with the device, the manufacturer will need to know which equipment was used, since the problem could be with the equipment itself. The same holds true for the individual(s) performing the process.

Section 820.75(b) applies to the performance of a process after the process has been validated. In contrast, § 820.75(a) relates to the initial validation of the process. The interval and frequency should be periodically evaluated for adequacy, especially during any evaluation or revalidation that occurs in accordance with the requirements in § 820.75(c).

ALSO SEE GHTF GUIDANCE, 4.9 PROCESS CONTROL

NOTES

SUBPART
H

Acceptance
Activities

 FDA QUALITY SYSTEM REGULATION—1996

§ 820.80 Receiving, in-process, and finished device acceptance

§ 820.80(a) *General.* Each manufacturer shall establish and maintain procedures for acceptance activities. Acceptance activities include inspections, tests, or other verification activities.

1978: § 820.20(a)(2) QUALITY ASSURANCE PROGRAM REQUIREMENTS

 ANSI/ISO/ASQC Q9001-1994

4.10 Inspection and testing

4.10.1 General

The supplier shall establish and maintain documented procedures for inspection and testing activities in order to verify that the specified requirements for the product are met. The required inspection and testing, and the records to be established, shall be detailed in the quality plan or documented procedures.

4.6.4 Verification of purchased product

4.6.4.1 Supplier verification at subcontractor's premises

Where the supplier proposes to verify purchased product at the subcontractor's premises, the supplier shall specify verification arrangements and the method of product release in the purchasing documents.

RECEIVING, IN-PROCESS, AND FINISHED
DEVICE ACCEPTANCE

125

4.6.4.2 Customer verification of subcontracted product

Where specified in the contract, the supplier's customer or the customer's representative shall be afforded the right to verify at the subcontractor's premises and the supplier's premises that subcontracted product conforms to specified requirements. Such verification shall not be used by the supplier as evidence of effective control of quality by the subcontractor.

Verification by the customer shall not absolve the supplier of the responsibility to provide acceptable product, nor shall it preclude subsequent rejection by the customer.

4.7 Control of customer-supplied product

The supplier shall establish and maintain documented procedures for the control of verification, storage, and maintenance of customer-supplied product provided for incorporation into the supplies or for related activities. Any such product that is lost, damaged, or is otherwise unsuitable for use shall be recorded and reported to the customer (see 4.16).

Verification by the supplier does not absolve the customer of the responsibility to provide acceptable product.

 **FDA GUIDANCE**

§ 820.80 Receiving, in-process, and finished device acceptance

The intent of § 820.50 is to ensure that device manufacturers select only those suppliers, contractors, and consultants who have the capability to provide quality product and services. As with finished devices, quality cannot be inspected or tested into products or services. Rather, the quality of a product or service is established during the design of that product or service and is achieved through proper control of the manufacture of that product or the performance of that service. Section 820.50 thus mandates that products be manufactured and services be performed under appropriate quality assurance procedures. Finished device manufacturers are required under § 820.50 to establish the requirements for, and document the capability of, suppliers, contractors, and consultants to provide quality products and services.

Section 820.80 is specific to a device manufacturer's acceptance program. While finished device manufacturers are required to assess the capability of suppliers, contractors, and consultants to provide quality products and services, inspections and tests and other verification tools are also an important part of ensuring that components and finished devices conform to approved specifications. The extent of incoming acceptance activities can be based, in part, on the degree to which the supplier has demonstrated a capability to provide quality products or services. An appropriate product and services quality assurance program includes a combination of assessment techniques, including inspection and test.

FDA believes that it is essential for the manufacturer to maintain records that provide evidence that the product has gone through the defined acceptance activities. These records must clearly show whether the product has passed or failed the acceptance activities according to the defined acceptance criteria. Where product fails to pass acceptance activities, the procedures for control of nonconforming product must be implemented, to include investigations where defined. If the acceptance records are not clear about how the product failed, then the manufacturer may end up duplicating the acceptance activities in order to perform appropriate investigations.

 **GHTF GUIDANCE**

4.10 Inspection and testing

4.10.1 General

No particular guidance was believed to be necessary for this section.

4.6.4 Verification of purchased product

If the supplier's procedures under 4.6.1–4.6.3 are described and documented in sufficient detail, they will provide satisfactory evidence that purchased product meets specified requirements.

If not, the supplier may find it difficult to satisfy the inquiries of customers or certification bodies. In such cases, the supplier may have to arrange for the customer/certification body to verify directly the subcontractor's product and/or processes.

4.7 Control of customer-supplied product

"Customer-supplied product" is product owned by the customer and furnished to the supplier. The supplier, upon delivery, accepts responsibilities for prevention from damage, and for identification, maintenance, storage, handling, and use while that product is in the supplier's possession.

For parts or medical devices provided by the customer to the supplier, the responsibility for their conformity to an agreed specification lies with the customer. However, the supplier should not knowingly incorporate nonconforming parts into any medical devices supplied to the customer.

FDA QUALITY SYSTEM REGULATION—1996

§ 820.80(b) Receiving acceptance activities

Each manufacturer shall establish and maintain procedures for acceptance of incoming product.

- Incoming product shall be inspected, tested, or otherwise verified as conforming to specified requirements.
- Acceptance or rejection shall be documented.

1978: § 820.80 COMPONENTS

ANSI/ISO/ASQC Q9001-1994

4.10.2 Receiving inspection and testing

4.10.2.1 The supplier shall ensure that incoming product is not used or processed (except in the circumstances described in 4.10.2.3) until it has been inspected or otherwise verified as conforming to specified requirements. Verification of the specified requirements shall be in accordance with the quality plan and/or documented procedures.

4.10.2.2 In determining the amount and nature of receiving inspection, consideration shall be given to the amount of control exercised at the subcontractor's premises and the recorded evidence of conformance provided.

4.10.2.3 Where incoming product is released for urgent production purposes prior to verification, it shall be positively identified and recorded (see 4.16) in order to permit immediate recall and replacement in the event of nonconformity to specified requirements.

FDA GUIDANCE

§ 820.80(b) Receiving acceptance activities

FDA has permitted manufacturers to use incoming items that had not yet been proven acceptable for use, provided that the manufacturer maintained control of the unapproved items and could retrieve the product that contained the unapproved items *before* distribution. FDA emphasizes that while the product can be used in production prior to verification, however, it *cannot* be distributed prior to verification. FDA does not permit the distribution of unapproved product through an urgent use provision, because all finished devices must comply with § 820.80(d) before they are released for distribution.

GHTF GUIDANCE

4.10.2 Receiving inspection and testing

4.10.2.1 Receiving inspection is one means for the supplier to verify that subcontractors have fulfilled their contractual obligations relating to quality and that procured items entering the supplier's facilities fulfill specified requirements for quality.

4.10.2.2 This clause in ISO 9001 does not imply that incoming items have to be inspected and tested by the supplier, if the necessary confidence in the product (including service) can be obtained by other defined procedures.

The supplier's procedures or quality plan should specify the means of verifying that shipments received are in accordance with specifications, are complete, have the proper identity, and are undamaged. The procedures should also include provisions for verifying that incoming items, materials, or services are accompanied by supporting documentation as, and if, required (e.g., certificates of analysis, test results). Appropriate action in the event of nonconformities should be specified. Analysis of past receiving inspection data, in-plant rejection history, or customer complaints can influence the supplier's decisions regarding the need to reassess a subcontractor.

4.10.2.3 The supplier's procedures should define responsibilities and authority of personnel who may allow incoming product(s) to be used without prior demonstration of conformance to specified requirements for quality. The supplier's procedures should also define how such product(s) will be positively identified and controlled in the event that subsequent inspection finds nonconformities.

 # FDA QUALITY SYSTEM REGULATION—1996

§ 820.80(c) In-process acceptance activities

Each manufacturer shall establish and maintain acceptance procedures, where appropriate, to ensure that specified requirements for in-process product are met. Such procedures shall ensure that in-process product is controlled until the required inspection and tests or other verification activities have been completed, or necessary approvals are received, and are documented.

1978: § 820.20(a)(2) QUALITY ASSURANCE PROGRAM REQUIREMENTS

 # ANSI/ISO/ASQC Q9001-1994

4.10.3 In-process inspection and testing

The supplier shall:

a)   inspect and test the product as required by the quality plan and/or documented procedures;

b)   hold product until the required inspection and tests have been completed or necessary reports have been received and verified, except when product is released under positive-recall procedures (see 4.10.2.3). Release under positive-recall procedures shall not preclude the activities outlined in 4.10.3a.

FDA GUIDANCE

§ 820.80(c) In-process acceptance activities

FDA acknowledges that in-process acceptance activities may not be necessary or possible for every device, for example, medical socks. Further, the requirement states that in-process product must be *controlled* until the required inspection and test, or other verification activities, have been performed. This will permit manufacturers to use, under defined conditions and procedures, product that has not completed the acceptance activities described in § 820.80(b) and (c). This does not means that manufacturers can ignore these requirements because they must be completed in order to comply with § 820.80(d), which must be satisfied before devices are released for distribution.

GHTF GUIDANCE

4.10.3 In-process inspection and testing

In-process inspection and testing applies to all forms of products, including services. It allows early recognition of nonconformities and timely disposition of the nonconforming items.

Where appropriate, statistical control techniques should be used to identify trends for both product and process before nonconformities actually occur.

The supplier's procedures or quality plan should ensure the objectivity of the inspection and test results, including situations where in-process inspection is carried out by production personnel.

Early identification of nonconformities, before arriving at the final inspection stage, increases the efficiency of the entire operation by avoiding further processing of nonconforming items.

§ 820.80(d) Final acceptance activities

Each manufacturer shall establish and maintain procedures for finished device acceptance to ensure that each production run, lot, or batch of finished devices meets acceptance criteria.

- Finished devices shall be held in quarantine or otherwise adequately controlled until released.
- Finished devices shall not be released for distribution until:
  (1) the activities required in the DMR are completed;
  (2) the associated data and documentation is reviewed;
  (3) the release is authorized by the signature of a designated individual(s); and
  (4) the authorization is dated.

1978: § 820.160 FINISHED DEVICE INSPECTION

 ANSI/ISO/ASQC Q9001-1994

4.10.4 Final inspection and testing

The supplier shall carry out all final inspection and testing in accordance with the quality plan and/or documented procedures to complete the evidence of conformance of the finished product to the specified requirements.

The quality plan and/or documented procedures for final inspection and testing shall require that all specified inspection and tests, including those specified either on receipt of product or in-process, have been carried out and that the results meet specified requirements.

No product shall be dispatched until all the activities specified in the quality plan and/or documented procedures have been satisfactorily completed and the associated data and documentation are available and authorized.

FDA GUIDANCE

§ 820.80(d) Final acceptance activities

Manufacturers must establish and maintain procedures for finished device acceptance to ensure that each production run, lot, or batch of finished devices meets specified requirements. Manufacturers have the flexibility to choose a combination of methods, including finished device inspection and test, provided such methods will accomplish the required result.

FDA believes that it is important for the person responsible for release to have personally documented and dated that release. This can be accomplished through use of an inspection stamp, if the stamp is controlled as discussed above under § 820.40, "Document controls."

GHTF GUIDANCE

4.10.4 Final inspection and testing

Final inspection involves the activities (examination, inspection, measurement, or test) upon which the final release of product (including service) is based with respect to specified characteristics. The specified requirements forming the basis of final inspection and test should include all designated release characteristics. These should be directly related to the type of medical device involved and its intended use. Final testing may include, where practical, testing under simulated or actual conditions of use of products selected from a lot or batch.

In the case of equipment which is assembled and/or installed at the user's premises, the final inspection and testing can only be carried out after the completion of assembly/installation. In such cases, the final inspection and test may not be carried out by the supplier, but the supplier should ensure the availability of all necessary information about the inspection and test procedure and the results expected.

FDA QUALITY SYSTEM REGULATION—1996

§ 820.80(e) Acceptance records

Each manufacturer shall document acceptance activities required by this part.

- These records shall include:

    (1) the acceptance activities performed;

    (2) the dates acceptance activities are performed;

    (3) the results;

    (4) the signature of the individual(s) conducting the acceptance activities; and

    (5) where appropriate the equipment used.

- These records shall be part of the device history record.

1978: § 820.20(a)(2) QUALITY ASSURANCE PROGRAM REQUIREMENTS AND § 820.161 CRITICAL DEVICE, FINISHED DEVICE INSPECTION

 ANSI/ISO/ASQC Q9001-1994

4.10.5 Inspection and test records

The supplier shall establish and maintain records which provide evidence that the product has been inspected and/or tested. These records shall show clearly whether the product has passed or failed the inspections and/or tests according to defined acceptance criteria. Where the product fails to pass any inspection and/or test, the procedures for control of nonconforming product shall apply (see 4.13).

Records shall identify the inspection authority responsible for the release of product (see 4.16).

ALSO SEE ISO/DIS 13485:1996, 4.10.5 INSPECTION AND TEST RECORDS

 **FDA GUIDANCE**

§ 820.80(e) Acceptance records

It may not be necessary to document every piece of equipment used in acceptance activities. For some critical operations and testing, however, identification of the equipment used will be imperative for proper investigations into nonconforming product.

 **GHTF GUIDANCE**

4.10.5 Inspection and test records

The supplier's inspection and test records should facilitate assessment of products having fulfilled the requirements for quality. Helpful supporting evidence may be available from records of other inspections and tests (e.g., raw materials, in-process). Regulatory requirements and product liability should also be taken into consideration.

Methods of recording the results of inspections and tests include:

—documentation regarding the product;

—electronic records, and

—separate test reports.

As applicable, records may:

—identify the inspection/test procedure(s) and revision level used (see also 4.5);

—identify the test equipment used;

—be signed and dated by the person responsible for the inspection or test;

—clearly identify the number of items examined and the number accepted;

—record the disposition of any items failing inspection or test, and the reasons for failure.

Final product release should be authorized by the signature of a designated person.

FDA QUALITY SYSTEM REGULATION—1996

§ 820.86 Acceptance status

Each manufacturer shall identify by suitable means the acceptance status of product, to indicate the conformance or nonconformance of these items with acceptance criteria. The identification of acceptance status shall be maintained throughout manufacturing, packaging, labeling, installation, and servicing of the product to ensure that only products which have passed the required acceptance activities are distributed, used, or installed.

1978: § 820.80(b) STORAGE AND HANDLING OF COMPONENTS AND § 820.160 FINISHED DEVICE INSPECTION

 **ANSI/ISO/ASQC Q9001-1994**

4.12 Inspection and test status

The inspection and test status of product shall be identified by suitable means, which indicate the conformance or nonconformance of product with regard to inspection and tests performed. The identification of inspection and test status shall be maintained, as defined in the quality plan and/or documented procedures, throughout production, installation, and servicing of the product to ensure that only product that has passed the required inspections and tests [or released under an authorized concession (see 4.13.2)] is dispatched, used, or installed.

 FDA GUIDANCE

§ 820.86 Acceptance status

Inspection and test status may be identified by any method that will achieve the result. This might include acceptable computerized identification or markings.

 **GHTF GUIDANCE**

4.12 Inspection and test status

The supplier's quality system and procedures should ensure that required inspections and tests are performed. The system should provide a way of knowing the product (including service) status. Status may be indicated by marking or tagging or signing, either physically or by electronic means. Status should indicate whether a product has not been inspected, has been inspected and rejected and on hold awaiting decision, or has been inspected and rejected. Separate physical location of these categories of product units is often the most certain method of assuring both the status and accurate disposition. However, in an automated environment accurate disposition may equally be achieved by other means, such as a computer database.

NOTES

NOTES

NOTES

SUBPART

Nonconforming Product

FDA QUALITY SYSTEM REGULATION—1996

§ 820.90 Nonconforming product

§ 820.90(a) Control of nonconforming product

Each manufacturer shall establish and maintain procedures to control product that does not conform to specified requirements.

- The procedures shall address the identification, documentation, evaluation, segregation, and disposition of nonconforming product.
- The evaluation of nonconformance shall include a determination of the need for an investigation and notification of the persons or organizations responsible for the nonconformance.
- The evaluation and any investigation shall be documented.

1978: § 820.161 CRITICAL DEVICE, FINISHED DEVICE INSPECTION

ANSI/ISO/ASQC Q9001-1994

4.13 Control of nonconforming product

4.13.1 General

The supplier shall establish and maintain documented procedures to ensure that product that does not conform to specified requirements is prevented from unintended use or installation.

This control shall provide for identification, documentation, evaluation, segregation (when practical), disposition of nonconforming product, and for notification to the functions concerned.

FDA GUIDANCE

§ 820.90 Nonconforming product

§ 820.90(a) Control of nonconforming product

First, the manufacturer must establish procedures to "control" nonconforming product. Second, the procedures shall "address the identification, documentation, evaluation, segregation, and disposition of nonconforming product," which gives the manufacturers the flexibility to define how they are going to "control" products that are nonconforming. Third, the evaluation process addressed in the procedure "shall include a determination of the need for an investigation." Therefore, the procedures will need to set forth the manufacturer's SOP on when investigations will take place and provisions for trending and/or monitoring the situation in the future. Fourth, "the evaluation and any investigation shall be documented" includes the explanations for not performing investigations and how nonconformances will be trended and/or monitored.

GHTF GUIDANCE

4.13 Control of nonconforming product

4.13.1 General

When any intermediate or final product (including service) is found (e.g., by test or inspection) not to conform to the technical specifications, inadvertent use or installation should be prevented. This is applicable to nonconforming product occurring in the supplier's own production as well as nonconforming product received by the supplier. Procedures are established and maintained by the supplier for the following purposes:

—to determine and document which product units are involved in the nonconformity, for example, what production time interval, or production machines, or product lots are involved;

—to mark the nonconforming product units to make sure that they can be distinguished from conforming product units (see 4.12);

—to evaluate and document the nature of the nonconformity;

—to consider the alternatives for disposition of the nonconforming product units, to decide what disposition should be made, and to record this disposition;

—to control (e.g., by physical segregation) the movements, storage, and subsequent processing of the nonconforming product consistent with the disposition decision;

—to notify other functions that may be affected by the nonconformity, including, where appropriate, the purchaser.

An important element in addressing nonconformities is to give to all appropriate personnel the freedom to identify nonconforming items, activities, and processes and encouragement to suggest improvements.

Any product returned to the supplier should be treated as nonconforming product until it has satisfied a documented acceptance procedure.

Before returned medical devices which may have been contaminated with biological material are handled, they should be decontaminated according to appropriate, approved procedures.

 FDA QUALITY SYSTEM REGULATION—1996

§ 820.90(b)(1) Nonconformity review and disposition

Each manufacturer shall establish and maintain procedures that define the responsibility for review and the authority for the disposition of nonconforming product.

- The procedures shall set forth the review and disposition process.
- Disposition of nonconforming product shall be documented.
- Documentation shall include the justification for use of nonconforming product and the signature of the individual(s) authorizing the use.

§ 820.90(b)(2). Each manufacturer shall establish and maintain procedures for rework, to include retesting and reevaluation of the nonconforming product after rework, to ensure that the product meets its current approved specifications. Rework and reevaluation activities, including a determination of any adverse effect from the rework upon the product, shall be documented in the device history record.

1978: § 820.116 CRITICAL DEVICE, REPROCESSING OF DEVICES OR COMPONENTS

 # ANSI/ISO/ASQC Q9001-1994

4.13.2 Review and disposition of nonconforming product

The responsibility for review and authority for the disposition of nonconforming product shall be defined.

Nonconforming product shall be reviewed in accordance with documented procedures. It may be

a)   reworked to meet the specified requirements,
b)   accepted with or without repair by concession,
c)   regraded for alternative applications, or
d)   rejected or scrapped.

Where required by the contract, the proposed use or repair of product (see 4.13.2b) which does not conform to specified requirements shall be reported for concession to the customer or customer's representative. The description of the nonconformity that has been accepted, and of repairs, shall be recorded to denote the actual condition (see 4.16).

Repaired and/or reworked product shall be reinspected in accordance with the quality plan and/or documented procedures.

ALSO SEE ISO/DIS 13485:1996, 4.13.2 REVIEW AND DISPOSITION OF NONCONFORMING PRODUCT

FDA GUIDANCE

§ 820.90(b)(1) Nonconformity review and disposition

FDA believes that proper disposition of nonconforming product is essential for ensuring the safety and effectiveness of devices. Manufacturers have made determinations that nonconforming product may be used, which has resulted in defective devices being distributed. Thus, although it may be appropriate at times to use nonconforming products, the disposition process must be adequately controlled. Therefore, the disposition and justification for concessions must be documented. Justification should be based on scientific evidence, which a manufacturer should be prepared to provide upon request. Concessions should be closely monitored and not become accepted practice.

Section 820.90(b)(2) governs rework when it is chosen as a method of disposition and requires that a determination of any adverse effect of the rework upon the product be made, whether there is "repeated" rework or not. Such a determination must be made with any rework, given the potentially harmful effect rework could have on the product.

 **GHTF GUIDANCE**

4.13.2 Review and disposition of nonconforming product

It is suggested that nonconformity disposition decisions made by the supplier take into consideration the six purposes listed under 4.13.1, in relationship to the risk of failure to meet the purchaser's requirements. Actions a, b, c, d in ISO 9001 all carry degrees of risk.

Concessions or changes in specification should be processed in accordance with documented procedures. If a product is allowed to be released under concession or is reworked, this should be recorded in the Device History Record (see 4.16). Any concession should be adequately justified, and the justification should be recorded.

NOTES

NOTES

NOTES

Corrective and Preventive Action

 FDA QUALITY SYSTEM REGULATION—1996

§ 820.100 Corrective and preventive action

§ 820.100(a) Each manufacturer shall establish and maintain procedures for implementing corrective and preventive action. The procedures shall include requirements for:

(1) Analyzing processes, work operations, concessions, quality audit reports, quality records, service records, complaints, returned product, and other sources of quality data to identify existing and potential causes of nonconforming product, or other quality problems. Appropriate statistical methodology shall be employed where necessary to detect recurring quality problems;

(2) Investigating the cause of nonconformities relating to product, processes, and the quality system;

(3) Identifying the action(s) needed to correct and prevent recurrence of nonconforming product and other quality problems;

(4) Verifying or validating the corrective and preventive action to ensure that such action is effective and does not adversely affect the finished device;

(5) Implementing and recording changes in methods and procedures needed to correct and prevent identified quality problems;

(6) Ensuring that information related to quality problems or nonconforming product is disseminated to those directly responsible for assuring the quality of such product or the prevention of such problems; and

(7) Submitting relevant information on identified quality problems, as well as corrective and preventive actions, for management review.

§ 820.100(b). All activities required under this section, and their results, shall be documented.

1978: § 820.20(a)(3) QUALITY ASSURANCE PROGRAM REQUIREMENTS AND § 820.162 FAILURE INVESTIGATION

ANSI/ISO/ASQC Q9001-1994

4.14 Corrective and preventive action

4.14.1 General

The supplier shall establish and maintain documented procedures for implementing corrective and preventive action.

Any corrective or preventive action taken to eliminate the causes of actual or potential nonconformities shall be to a degree appropriate to the magnitude of problems and commensurate with the risks encountered.

The supplier shall implement and record any changes to the documented procedures resulting from corrective and preventive action.

4.14.2 Corrective action

The procedures for corrective action shall include:

a) the effective handling of customer complaints and reports of product nonconformities;

b) investigation of the cause of nonconformities relating to product, process, and quality system, and recording the results of the investigation (see 4.16);

c) determination of the corrective action needed to eliminate the cause of nonconformities;

d) application of controls to ensure that corrective action is taken and that it is effective.

4.14.3 Preventive action

The procedures for preventive action shall include:

a) the use of appropriate sources of information such as processes and work operations which affect product quality, concessions, audit results, quality records, service reports, and customer complaints to detect, analyze, and eliminate potential causes of nonconformities;

b) determination of the steps needed to deal with any problems requiring preventive action;

c) initiation of preventive action and application of controls to ensure that it is effective;

d) ensuring that relevant information on actions taken is submitted for management review (see 4.1.3).

ALSO SEE ISO/DIS 13485:1996, 4.14 CORRECTIVE AND PREVENTIVE ACTION AND 4.14.1 GENERAL

 **FDA GUIDANCE**

§ 820.100 Corrective and preventive action

It is essential that manufacturers establish procedures for implementing corrective and preventive action. The procedures must include provisions for the remaining requirements in this section. These procedures must provide for control and action to be taken on devices distributed, and those not yet distributed, that are suspected of having potential nonconformities. The degree of corrective and preventive action taken to eliminate or minimize actual or potential nonconformities must be appropriate to the magnitude of the problem and commensurate with the risks encountered. FDA cannot dictate in a regulation the degree of action that should be taken because each circumstance will be different, but FDA does expect the manufacturer to develop procedures for assessing the risk, the actions that need to be taken for different levels of risk, and how to correct or prevent the problem from recurring, depending on that risk assessment.

Any death, even if the manufacturer attributes it to user error, will be considered relevant by FDA and will potentially have a high risk associated with it. User error is still considered to be a nonconformity, because human factors and other similar tools should have been considered during the design phase of the device. FDA acknowledges that a manufacturer cannot possibly foresee every single potential misuse during the design of a device, but when the manufacturer becomes aware of misuse, the corrective and preventive action requirements should be implemented to determine if redesign of the device or labeling changes may be necessary.

The inclusion of quality audits as a valuable feedback mechanism for the manufacturer does not conflict with FDA's policy of not reviewing internal quality audits. Internal audits are valuable and necessary tools for the manufacturer to evaluate the quality system. The audit reports should be used to analyze the entire quality system and provide feedback into the system to close the feedback loop, so that corrective or preventive actions can be taken where necessary. FDA will review the corrective and preventive action procedures and activities performed in conformance with those procedures without reviewing the internal audit reports. Preventive and corrective actions, to include the activities and documentation of such action, that result from internal audits and management reviews are *not* covered under § 820.180(c). Manufacturers will be required to make this information readily available to an FDA investigator so that the investigator may properly assess the manufacturer's compliance with these quality system requirements.

The requirements in this section are broader than the requirement for investigations under § 820.198, because it requires that nonconforming product discovered before or after distribution be investigated to the degree commensurate with the significance and risk of the nonconformity. At times a very in-depth investigation will be necessary, while at other times a simple investigation, followed by trend analysis or other appropriate tools, will be acceptable. In addition, in contrast to § 820.198, the requirement in this section applies to process and quality system nonconformities, as well as product nonconformities. For example, if a molding process with its known capabilities has a normal 5 percent rejection rate and that rate rises to 10 percent, an investigation into the nonconformance of the process must be performed. This section also addresses problems within the quality system itself. Correction and prevention of unacceptable quality system practices should result in fewer nonconformities related to product. For example, manufacturers should identify and correct improper personnel training, the failure to follow procedures, and inadequate procedures, among other things.

GHTF GUIDANCE

4.14 Corrective and preventive action

4.14.1 General

It is important that the causes of detected (or potential) nonconformities be promptly identified in order that a program to prevent recurrence (or occurrence) may be developed. These causes may include:

—failures, malfunctions, or nonconformities in incoming materials, processes, tools, equipment, or facilities in which products are processed, stored, or handled, including the equipment and systems therein;

—inadequate or nonexistent procedures and documentation;

—noncompliance with procedures;

—inadequate process control;

—poor scheduling;

—lack of training;

—inadequate working conditions;

—inadequate resources (human or material);

—inherent process variability.

The conditions resulting from these causes may be revealed by analysis of both internal and external observations.
    Internal observations may include:

—inspection and test records;

—nonconformity records;

—observations during process monitoring;

—audit observations;

—observations and reports by the supplier's personnel;

—subcontract problems;

—management review results.

    External observations ("feedback") may include:

—reports from the marketing function;

—reports from authorized representatives;

—service records;

—customer complaints or reports;

—returned product;

—solicited information on new or modified products;

—reports from regulatory authorities;

—published literature.

Regulations may place requirements on suppliers to monitor the use of their products and inform regulatory authorities of certain defined experience in use.

4.14.2 Corrective action

The supplier's procedures should clearly establish responsibility for taking corrective action, how this action will be carried out, and verification of the effectiveness of the corrective action. An important element in the program is the dissemination of quality problem information to those directly responsible for ensuring quality.

The procedures for dealing with nonconformities discovered in product which has already been shipped as satisfactory can include, among others:

—investigations to establish whether the nonconformity is an isolated or a chronic problem;

if necessary, taking such actions as:

- withholding products available for sale;
- withdrawing products from circulation;
- giving advice to customers: this may take the form of checks to be carried out before use, providing additional guidance on the use of the product or for the replacement of certain products;
- in extreme cases, the recall of products.

COMPLAINTS

Any complaint received by the supplier on a product which either i) fails to conform with its specification, or ii) conforms with its specification but nevertheless causes a problem in use, should fall under the complaints system. For instance, a complaint with a conforming product may be caused by a fault in the design.

The documented complaints system should cover the following:

—establishing responsibility for operating the system;

—evaluation of the complaint;

—records and statistical summaries, enabling the major causes of complaints to be determined;

—any corrective action;

—segregation and disposition, or reprocessing, of customer returns and faulty stock (special attention may need to be given to decontamination);

—filing of customer correspondence and other relevant records; the retention time for these should be defined.

The documentation of complaint investigations should contain enough information to show that the complaint was properly reviewed. For example: a determination of whether there was an actual product failure to perform per specifications; whether the product was being used to treat or diagnose a patient; whether a death, injury, or serious illness was involved; the relationship, if any, to the reported incident or adverse event. An investigation record would typically include:

1. the name of the product;
2. the date the complaint was received;
3. any control number used;
4. the name and address of the complainant;
5. the nature of the complaint;
6. The results of the investigation, including:
   - the corrective action taken
   - the justification, if no action is taken
   - the dates of the investigation
   - the name of the investigator
   - the reply (if any) to the complainant.

Where the technical staff who are responsible for an investigation are located at a site other than the place of manufacture of the medical device, the supplier should copy the records of the complaint and the investigation to the manufacturing plant, so that the staff at that plant can be fully informed of the events.

ADVISORY NOTICES AND PRODUCT RECALL

The nature and seriousness of the fault, the intended use of the product, and the consequential potential for patient injury or harm, will determine whether it will be necessary to issue an advisory notice, to institute a recall, and/or to report to local or national authorities. These factors will also determine the speed and extent of the action.

A person, with nominated deputies to cover for periods of absence, should be designated to coordinate the issue of each advisory notice or recall and the consequent actions.

The procedures for generating, authorizing, and issuing an advisory notice or recall should specify:

—the management arrangements that enable the procedure to be activated, even in the absence of key personnel;

—the level of management that determines that the procedure should be initiated, and the method of determining the affected products;

—the possible necessity to report to local or national authorities, the points of contact, and methods of communication between the supplier and national authorities.

An advisory notice or recall should provide:

—the description of the medical device and model designation;
—the serial numbers or other identification (for instance, batch or lot numbers) of the medical devices concerned;
—the reason for the issue of the notice/recall;
—advice of possible hazards and consequent action to be taken.

The progress of a recall should be monitored and amounts of product received should be reconciled.

4.14.3 Preventive action

Documented procedures addressing the actions described in this subclause of ISO 9001 should be developed by the supplier. In particular, they should establish responsibility for taking preventive action, how this action is to be implemented, and the verification of the effectiveness of the preventive action.

NOTES

NOTES

SUBPART K

Labeling and Packaging Control

 FDA QUALITY SYSTEM REGULATION—1996

§ 820.120 Device labeling

Each manufacturer shall establish and maintain procedures to control labeling activities.

§ 820.120(a) Label integrity

Labels shall be printed and applied so as to remain legible and affixed during the customary conditions of processing, storage, handling, distribution, and where appropriate use.

§ 820.120(b) Labeling inspection

Labeling shall not be released for storage or use until a designated individual(s) has examined the labeling for accuracy including, where applicable, the correct expiration date, control number, storage instructions, handling instructions, and any additional processing instructions. The release, including the date and signature of the individual(s) performing the examination, shall be documented in the device history record.

§ 820.120(c) Labeling storage

Each manufacturer shall store labeling in a manner that provides proper identification and is designed to prevent mixups.

§ 820.120(d) Labeling operations

Each manufacturer shall control labeling and packaging operations to prevent labeling mixups. The label and labeling used for each production unit, lot, or batch shall be documented in the device history record.

§ 820.120(e) Control number

Where a control number is required by § 820.65, that control number shall be on or shall accompany the device through distribution.

1978: § 820.120 DEVICE LABELING AND § 820.121 CRITICAL DEVICES, DEVICE LABELING

 **FDA GUIDANCE**

§ 820.120 Device labeling

This section is consistent with the requirements in the original CGMP. Section 820.120 relates specifically to labeling and its requirements are in addition to those in both § 820.80 and § 820.86. Further, FDA believes that the degree of detail in this section is necessary because these same requirements have been in place for 18 years, yet numerous recalls every year are the result of labeling errors or mixups.

The requirements do not preclude manufacturers from using automated readers where that process is followed by human oversight. A "designated individual" must examine, at a minimum, a representative sampling of all labels that have been checked by the automated readers. Further, automated readers are often programmed with only the base label and do not check specifics, such as control numbers and expiration dates, among other things, that are distinct for each label. The regulation requires that labeling be inspected for these items prior to release.

FDA QUALITY SYSTEM REGULATION—1996

§ 820.130 Device packaging

Each manufacturer shall ensure that device packaging and shipping containers are designed and constructed to protect the device from alteration or damage during the customary conditions of processing, storage, handling, and distribution.

1978: § 820.130 DEVICE PACKAGING

ANSI/ISO/ASQC Q9001-1994

4.15 Handling, storage, packaging, preservation, and delivery

4.15.1 General

The supplier shall establish and maintain documented procedures for handling, storage, packaging, preservation, and delivery of product.

ALSO SEE ISO/DIS 13485:1996, 4.15 HANDLING, STORAGE, PACKAGING, PRESERVATION AND DELIVERY AND 4.15.1 GENERAL

4.15.4 Packaging

The supplier shall control packing, packaging, and marking processes (including materials used) to the extent necessary to ensure conformance to specified requirements.

ALSO SEE ISO/DIS 13485:1996, 4.15.4 PACKAGING

FDA GUIDANCE

§ 820.130 Device packaging

FDA believes that any intentional tampering would not be covered because the requirement states "during customary conditions."

 **GHTF GUIDANCE**

4.15 Handling, storage, packaging, preservation, and delivery

4.15.1 General

The supplier's system for handling, storage, packaging, and delivery of materials should provide proper planning, control, and documentation. This includes in-process materials and finished product.

4.15.4 Packaging

The packaging of medical devices is intended to provide appropriate protection against damage, deterioration, or contamination during storage and transportation up to the point of use. The various forms of storage and the types of transportation that might be encountered therefore should be considered, and the effectiveness of the packaging checked.

Where the packaging of the product has been subcontracted, it remains the responsibility of the supplier to ensure that the requirements of 4.15.4 are met.

LABELING

The content of labels may be specified in regulations, general standards, or product standards. Where product is to be supplied to countries with different languages, and the language to be used on the labels has been agreed, it is advisable for the label translations to be checked by a person whose native language is the agreed language and who has some technical knowledge of the product. Translation problems can be reduced by the use of internationally agreed symbols.

Where appropriate, a record should be retained of the identity of the person who confirms that the correct label(s) has been fixed to and supplied with the medical devices.

The risk of labeling and packaging errors may be minimized by the introduction of appropriate controls such as:

—segregation of packaging and labeling operations from other manufacturing (or other packaging and labeling) operations;
—avoidance of packaging and labeling product of similar appearance in close proximity;
—line identification;
—application of line clearance procedures;

—the destruction of unused batch coded materials on completion of packaging and labeling;

—use of roll feed labels;

—use of a known number of labels and reconciliation of usage;

—on-line batch coding;

—use of electronic code encoders/readers and label counters;

—use of labels designed to provide clear product differentiation;

—inspection of label content before use;

—proper storage of labels in areas of restricted access.

NOTES

NOTES

SUBPART
L

Handling, Storage, Distribution, and Installation

FDA QUALITY SYSTEM REGULATION—1996

§ 820.140 Handling

Each manufacturer shall establish and maintain procedures to ensure that mixups, damage, deterioration, contamination, or other adverse effects to product do not occur during handling.

1978: § 820.80(b) STORAGE AND HANDLING OF COMPONENTS

ANSI/ISO/ASQC Q9001-1994

4.15 Handling, storage, packaging, preservation, and delivery

4.15.1 General

The supplier shall establish and maintain documented procedures for handling, storage, packaging, preservation, and delivery of product.

4.15.2 Handling

The supplier shall provide methods of handling product that prevent damage or deterioration.

HANDLING

 **FDA GUIDANCE**

§ 820.140 Handling

These procedures are expected to ensure that mixups, damage, deterioration, contamination, or other adverse effects do not occur. The requirement applies to all stages of handling in which a manufacturer is involved, which may, in some cases, go beyond initial distribution.

 **GHTF GUIDANCE**

4.15.2 Handling

Careful planning and appropriate operating procedures help to ensure that the handling of incoming product, product in process, and completed or released medical devices does not jeopardize quality.

The supplier's method for handling materials should consider providing transportation units (such as pallets, containers, conveyors, vessels, tanks, pipelines, and vehicles) so that damage, deterioration, or contamination (due to vibration, shock, abrasion, corrosion, temperature variation, radiation, or any other conditions occurring during handling and storage) may be prevented. Maintenance of handling equipment is another factor to be considered.

FDA QUALITY SYSTEM REGULATION—1996

§ 820.150 Storage

§ 820.150(a). Each manufacturer shall establish and maintain procedures for the control of storage areas and stock rooms for product to prevent mixups, damage, deterioration, contamination, or other adverse effects pending use or distribution and to ensure that no obsolete, rejected, or deteriorated product is used or distributed. When the quality of product deteriorates over time, it shall be stored in a manner to facilitate proper stock rotation, and its condition shall be assessed as appropriate.

§ 820.150(b). Each manufacturer shall establish and maintain procedures that describe the methods for authorizing receipt from and dispatch to storage areas and stock rooms.

1978: § 820.80(b) STORAGE AND HANDLING OF COMPONENTS

 # ANSI/ISO/ASQC Q9001-1994

4.15 Handling, storage, packaging, preservation, and delivery

4.15.1 General

The supplier shall establish and maintain documented procedures for handling, storage, packaging, preservation, and delivery of product.

4.15.3 Storage

The supplier shall use designated storage areas or stock rooms to prevent damage or deterioration of product, pending use or delivery. Appropriate methods for authorizing receipt to and dispatch from such areas shall be stipulated.

In order to detect deterioration, the condition of product in stock shall be assessed at appropriate intervals.

4.15.5 Preservation

The supplier shall apply appropriate methods for preservation and segregation of product when the product is under the supplier's control.

FDA GUIDANCE

§ 820.150 Storage

Strict control over product in storage areas and stock rooms results in decreased distribution of nonconforming product. Thus, even where locked storage rooms are utilized, the procedures should detail, among other things, who is permitted access and what steps should be followed prior to removal.

GHTF GUIDANCE

4.15.3 Storage

The supplier should plan for suitable storage facilities, considering not only physical security but also environmental conditions (e.g., temperature and humidity). It may be appropriate to check periodically items in storage to detect possible deterioration.

The methods for marking and labeling should give legible, durable information in accordance with the specifications. Consideration may need to be given to administrative procedures for expiry dates, and stock rotation and lot segregation.

Orderly storage conditions enable rapid and accurate identification of stock and facilitate cleaning, while minimizing risk of damage. Storage management procedures should be reviewed by the person responsible for quality assurance.

Raw materials and products which have been rejected, recalled, or returned should be identified and may be placed in quarantine to prevent confusion with other materials. Access to materials in quarantine areas should be restricted to authorized persons. Release and disposition should be carried out according to a defined procedure.

4.15.5 Preservation

Shelf-life commences during manufacture and may be influenced by the conditions of storage. The identification of items with a limited shelf life, or which require special protection during storage, is important to ensure that such items are not issued if their shelf life has expired. The supplier should have means of informing the customer or user about any special storage conditions which may apply.

FDA QUALITY SYSTEM REGULATION—1996

§ 820.160 Distribution

§ 820.160(a). Each manufacturer shall establish and maintain procedures for control and distribution of finished devices to ensure that only those devices approved for release are distributed and that purchase orders are reviewed to ensure that ambiguities and errors are resolved before devices are released for distribution. Where a device's fitness for use or quality deteriorates over time, the procedures shall ensure that expired devices or devices deteriorated beyond acceptable fitness for use are not distributed.

1978: § 820.150 DISTRIBUTION

 ANSI/ISO/ASQC Q9001-1994

4.3 Contract review

4.3.1 General

The supplier shall establish and maintain documented procedures for contract review and for the coordination of these activities.

4.3.2 Review

Before submission of a tender, or at the acceptance of a contract or order (statement of requirement), the tender, contract, or order shall be reviewed by the supplier to ensure that:

a)   the requirements are adequately defined and documented; where no written statement of requirement is available for an order received by verbal means, the supplier shall ensure that the order requirements are agreed before their acceptance;

b)   any differences between the contract or accepted order requirements and those in the tender are resolved;

c)   the supplier has the capability to meet the contract or accepted order requirements.

4.3.3 Amendment to contract

The supplier shall identify how an amendment to a contract is made and correctly transferred to the functions concerned within the supplier's organization.

4.3.4 Records

Records of contract reviews shall be maintained (see 4.16).

NOTE 9 Channels for communication and interfaces with the customer's organization in these contract matters should be established.

 **GHTF GUIDANCE**

4.3 Contract review

4.3.1 General

4.3.2 Review

The importance of a thorough understanding of the purchaser's needs during the tendering stage at the formulation of the contract and in all subsequent stages cannot be overstated. Often dialogue will be necessary to achieve this understanding, that should clearly establish the purchaser's requirements as to the product, delivery, and other critical factors.

Medical devices may be supplied to customers via telephoned or written purchase orders, or on the receipt of a standing order. Such orders are often based on information supplied to the customer in the form of a sales catalogue. In some situations a documented contract may be agreed between the parties concerned. In all these circumstances a legally binding contract may be deemed to exist and the contract review process should be applied.

Contracts established to permit supply of product by Electronic Data Interchange need especially careful review in order to ensure that the subsequent automatic processes can be operated safely.

4.3.3 Amendment to contract

Amendments to contracts may be introduced by the customer (e.g., change of requirements) or by the supplier (e.g., inability to meet specification or dates). Changes introduced by the customer should be subjected to the same review procedure as new contracts. A documented system should exist for ensuring that changes are communicated to all affected parts of the supplier's organization. Changes introduced by the supplier should be agreed by the customer and this agreement should be documented.

4.3.4 Records

In most cases it should be sufficient for records to be kept to show that a review has taken place. In some cases, particularly where a contract has been amended, it may be advisable to keep more detailed records.

 # FDA QUALITY SYSTEM REGULATION—1996

§ 820.160(b). Each manufacturer shall maintain distribution records which include or refer to the location of:

(1) The name and address of the initial consignee;

(2) The identification and quantity of devices shipped;

(3) The date shipped; and

(4) Any control number(s) used.

1978: § 820.151 CRITICAL DEVICES, DISTRIBUTION RECORDS

 # ANSI/ISO/ASQC Q9001-1994

4.15 Handling, storage, packaging, preservation, and delivery

4.15.1 General

The supplier shall establish and maintain documented procedures for handling, storage, packaging, preservation, and delivery of product.

4.15.6 Delivery

The supplier shall arrange for the protection of the quality of product after final inspection and test. Where contractually specified, this protection shall be extended to include delivery to destination.

ALSO SEE ISO/DIS 13485:1996, 4.15.6 DELIVERY

FDA GUIDANCE

§ 820.160 Distribution

FDA agrees with the concepts underlying the contract review requirements of ISO 9001:1994, but believes these principles are already reflected in requirements in the regulation through sections such as § 820.50, "Purchasing controls," and 820.160, "Distribution." Therefore, the agency has not added a separate section on contract review.

If the manufacturer is required by § 820.65 to have control numbers, these must be recorded along with any control numbers voluntarily used. Logically, control numbers are used for traceability, so they should be recorded in the DHR distribution records. This section requires basic information needed for any class of product in order to conduct recalls or other corrective actions when necessary.

GHTF GUIDANCE

4.15.6 Delivery

The supplier should provide for protection of the quality of product during shipping and other phases of delivery. For some products, including services, delivery time is a critical factor. Consideration should be given to the various types of delivery and variations in environmental conditions that may be encountered. The traceability requirements of 4.8 may require the maintenance of distribution records.

DISTRIBUTION

§ 820.170 Installation

§ 820.170(a). Each manufacturer of a device requiring installation shall establish and maintain adequate installation and inspection instructions, and where appropriate test procedures.

- Instructions and procedures shall include directions for ensuring proper installation so that the device will perform as intended after installation.
- The manufacturer shall distribute the instructions and procedures with the device or otherwise make them available to the person(s) installing the device.

§ 820.170(b). The person installing the device shall ensure that the installation, inspection, and any required testing are performed in accordance with the manufacturer's instructions and procedures and shall document the inspection and any test results to demonstrate proper installation.

1978: § 820.152 INSTALLATION

SEE ANSI/ISO/ASQC Q9001-1994, 4.9 PROCESS CONTROL

ALSO SEE ISO/DIS 13485:1996, 4.9(E) INSTALLATION

 **FDA GUIDANCE**

§ 820.170 Installation

Persons who install medical devices have been regulated under the original CGMP under § 820.3(k), which describes a manufacturer as one who "assembles or processes a finished medical device," and continue to be regulated under this quality system regulation under § 820.3(o). Section 820.152 of the original CGMP discussed the manufacturer or its authorized representative and persons other than the manufacturer's representative. The new regulation eliminates that terminology. Under the revised requirement in § 820.170(a), the manufacturer establishes installation and inspection instructions, and, where appropriate, test procedures. The manufacturer distributes the instructions and

INSTALLATION

procedures with the device or makes them available to person(s) installing the device. Section 820.170(b) requires that the person(s) installing the device follow the instructions and procedures described in § 820.170(a) and document the activities described in the procedures and instructions to demonstrate proper installation.

Section 820.170(b) explicitly requires that the installation be performed according to the manufacturer's instructions, regardless of whether the installer is employed by or otherwise affiliated with the manufacturer. Section 820.170(b) requires records to be kept by whomever performs the installation to establish that the installation was performed according to the procedures. Such records will be available for FDA inspection. FDA does not expect the manufacturer of the finished device to maintain records of installation performed by those installers not affiliated with the manufacturer, but does expect the third-party installer or the user of the device to maintain such records.

FDA believes that making these requirements explicit in the regulation is necessary to ensure that devices are safe and effective and that they perform as intended after installation. FDA notes again that installers are considered to be manufacturers under the original CGMP regulation and that their records are, and will continue to be, subject to FDA inspections when the agency deems it necessary to review such records.

ALSO SEE GHTF GUIDANCE, 4.9 PROCESS CONTROL

NOTES

SUBPART M Records

 FDA QUALITY SYSTEM REGULATION—1996

§ 820.180 General requirements

All records required by this part shall be maintained at the manufacturing establishment or other location that is reasonably accessible to responsible officials of the manufacturer and to employees of FDA designated to perform inspections.

- Such records, including those not stored at the inspected establishment, shall be made readily available for review and copying by FDA employee(s).
- Such records shall be legible and shall be stored to minimize deterioration and to prevent loss.
- Those records stored in automated data processing systems shall be backed up.

§ 820.180(a) Confidentiality

Records deemed confidential by the manufacturer may be marked to aid FDA in determining whether information may be disclosed under the public information regulation in part 20 of this chapter.

§ 820.180(b) Record retention period

All records required by this part shall be retained for a period of time equivalent to the design and expected life of the device, but in no case less than 2 years from the date of release for commercial distribution by the manufacturer.

§ 820.180(c) Exceptions

This section does not apply to the reports required by § 820.20(c) Management review, § 820.22 Quality audits, and supplier audit reports used to meet the requirements of § 820.50(a) Evaluation of suppliers, contractors, and consultants, but does apply to procedures established under these provisions. Upon request of a designated employee of the FDA, an employee in management with executive responsibility shall certify in writing that the management reviews and quality audits required under this part, and supplier audits where applicable, have been performed and documented, the dates on which they were performed, and that any required corrective action has been undertaken.

1978: § 820.180 GENERAL REQUIREMENTS

 **FDA GUIDANCE**

§ 820.180 Records

Records must be kept in a location that is "reasonably accessible" to both the manufacturer and FDA investigators, and records must be made "readily available." FDA expects that such records will be made available during the course of an inspection. If a foreign manufacturer maintains records at remote locations, such records would be expected to be produced in one or two working days.

Records should be retained for a period equivalent to the design and expected life of the device, but in no case less than two years, whether the records specifically pertain to a particular device or not. Records, including quality records, are subject to the requirement. This is necessary because manufacturers need all such records when performing any type of investigation. For example, it may be very important to access the wording of a complaint-handling procedure at the time a particular complaint came in when investigating a trend or a problem that extends to several products or over an extended period of time.

Section 820.180(c) addresses which records FDA, as a matter of policy, will not request to review or copy during a routine inspection; such records include quality audit reports. FDA may request an employee in management with executive responsibility to certify in writing that the management reviews, quality audits, and supplier audits (where conducted) have been performed, among other things. FDA may also seek production of these reports in litigation under applicable procedural rules or by inspection warrant where access to the records is authorized by statute. FDA emphasizes that its policy of refraining from reviewing these reports extends only to the specific reports, not to the procedures required by the sections or to any other quality assurance records, which will be subject to review and copying.

§ 820.181 Device master record

Each manufacturer shall maintain device master records (DMRs). Each manufacturer shall ensure that each DMR is prepared and approved in accordance with § 820.40. The DMR for each type of device shall include, or refer to the location of, the following information:

§ 820.181(a). Device specifications including appropriate drawings, composition, formulation, component specifications, and software specifications;

§ 820.181(b). Production process specifications including the appropriate equipment specifications, production methods, production procedures, and production environment specifications;

§ 820.181(c). Quality assurance procedures and specifications including acceptance criteria and the quality assurance equipment to be used;

§ 820.181(d). Packaging and labeling specifications, including methods and processes used; and

1996:§ 820.181(e). Installation, maintenance, and servicing procedures and methods.

1978: § 820.181 DEVICE MASTER RECORD AND § 820.182 CRITICAL DEVICES, DEVICE MASTER RECORD

ALSO SEE ISO/DIS 13485:1996, 4.2.3 QUALITY PLANNING

 **FDA GUIDANCE**

§ 820.181 Device master record (DMR)

FDA believes that it is more important for manufacturers to construct a document structure that is workable and traceable than to worry about whether something is contained in one file as compared to another. The DMR is set up to contain or reference

the procedures and specifications that are current on the manufacturing floor. The DHF is meant to be more of a historical file
for utilization during investigations and continued design
efforts.

There are requirements for validation and verification pertaining to device processing that may be better kept in the DMR
instead of the DHF. The documentation of such verification and
validation activities relating to processes that are performed for
several different devices or types of devices can be placed or referenced in the location that best suits the manufacturer. Again, it
is more important that the manufacturer store and retrieve information in a workable manner, than keep such information in particular files.

FDA QUALITY SYSTEM REGULATION—1996

§ 820.184 Device history record

Each manufacturer shall maintain device history records (DHRs). Each manufacturer shall establish and maintain procedures to ensure that DHRs for each batch, lot, or unit are maintained to demonstrate that the device is manufactured in accordance with the DMR and the requirements of this part. The DHR shall include, or refer to the location of, the following information:

(a) The dates of manufacture;

(b) The quantity manufactured;

(c) The quantity released for distribution;

(d) The acceptance records which demonstrate the device is manufactured in accordance with the DMR;

(e) The primary identification label and labeling used for each production unit; and

(f) Any device identification(s) and control number(s) used.

1978: § 820.184 DEVICE HISTORY RECORD, § 820.185 CRITICAL DEVICES, DEVICE HISTORY RECORD, AND § 820.20(a)(1) QUALITY ASSURANCE PROGRAM REQUIREMENTS

 # FDA GUIDANCE

§ 820.184 Device history record (DHR)

The DHR is the actual production records for a particular device and should be able to show the processes, tests, rework, and so on that the device went through from the beginning of its manufacture through distribution.

§ 820.186 Quality system record

Each manufacturer shall maintain a quality system record (QSR).

- The QSR shall include, or refer to the location of, procedures and the documentation of activities required by this part that are not specific to a particular type of device(s), including but not limited to the records required by § 820.20.
- Each manufacturer shall ensure that the QSR is prepared and approved in accordance with § 820.40.

1978: § 820.180 GENERAL REQUIREMENTS

# FDA GUIDANCE

§ 820.186 Quality system record (QSR)

This section separates the procedures and documentation of activities that are not specific to a particular type of device from the device specific records.

§ 820.198 Complaint files

§ 820.198(a). Each manufacturer shall maintain complaint files. Each manufacturer shall establish and maintain procedures for receiving, reviewing, and evaluating complaints by a formally designated unit. Such procedures shall ensure that:

(1) All complaints are processed in a uniform and timely manner;

(2) Oral complaints are documented upon receipt; and

(3) Complaints are evaluated to determine whether the complaint represents an event which is required to be reported to the FDA under part 803 or 804 of this chapter, Medical Device Reporting.

§ 820.198(b). Each manufacturer shall review and evaluate all complaints to determine whether an investigation is necessary. When no investigation is made, the manufacturer shall maintain a record that includes the reason no investigation was made and the name of the individual responsible for the decision not to investigate.

§ 820.198(c). Any complaint involving the possible failure of a device, labeling, or packaging to meet any of its specifications shall be reviewed, evaluated, and investigated, unless such investigation has already been performed for a similar complaint and another investigation is not necessary.

§ 820.198(d). Any complaint that represents an event which must be reported to FDA under part 803 or 804 of this chapter shall be promptly reviewed, evaluated, and investigated by a designated individual(s) and shall be maintained in a separate portion of the complaint files or clearly identified. In addition to the information required by § 820.198(e), records of investigations under this paragraph shall include a determination of:

(1) Whether the device failed to meet specifications;

(2) Whether the device was being used for treatment or diagnosis; and

(3) The relationship, if any, of the device to the reported incident or adverse event.

§ 820.198(e). When an investigation is made under this section, a record of each investigation shall be maintained by the formally designated unit identified in paragraph (a) of this section. The record of investigation shall include:

(1) The name of the device;

(2) The date the complaint was received;

(3) Any device identification(s) and control number(s) used;

(4) The name, address, and phone number of the complainant;

(5) The nature and details of the complaint;

(6) The dates and results of the investigation;

(7) Any corrective action taken; and

(8) Any reply to the complainant.

§ 820.198(f). When the manufacturer's formally designated complaint unit is located at a site separate from the manufacturing establishment, the investigated complaint(s) and the record(s) of investigation shall be reasonably accessible to the manufacturing establishment.

§ 820.198(g). If a manufacturer's formally designated complaint unit is located outside of the United States, records required by this section shall be reasonably accessible in the United States at either:

(1) A location in the United States where the manufacturer's records are regularly kept; or

(2) The location of the initial distributor.

1978: § 820.198 COMPLAINT FILES

 **FDA GUIDANCE**

§ 820.198 Complaint files

Section 820.198(a) sets forth the general requirement for establishing and maintaining a complaint-handling procedure and includes a few items that the procedure needs to address. Section 820.198(b) discusses the initial review and evaluation of the complaints in order to determine if complaints are valid. It is important to note that this evaluation is not the same as a complaint investigation. The evaluation is performed to determine whether the information is truly a complaint or not and to determine whether the complaint needs to be investigated or not.

If the evaluation decision is not to investigate, the justification must be recorded. Section 820.198(c) then describes one subset of complaints that must be investigated, but explains that duplicative investigations are not necessary. In cases where an investigation would be duplicative, a reference to the original investigation is an acceptable justification for not conducting a second investigation.

Section 820.198(d) describes another subset of complaints that must be investigated (those that meet the MDR criteria) and the information that is necessary in the record of investigation of those types of complaints. Section 820.198(e) sets out the type of information that must be recorded whenever complaints are investigated. The information described in § 820.198(e)(1) through (e)(5) would most likely be attained earlier in order to perform the evaluation in § 820.198(b). This information need not be duplicated in the investigation report as long as the complaint and investigation report can be properly identified and tied together. Section 820.198(e)(1) through (e)(5) are considered to be basic information essential to any complaint investigation. If there is some reason that the information described in § 820.198(e) cannot be obtained, then the manufacturer should document the situation and explain the efforts made to ascertain the information. This will be considered to be acceptable as long as a reasonable and good faith effort was made. For example, a single phone call to a hospital would not be considered by FDA to be a reasonable, good faith effort to obtain information.

Section 820.198(f) is the same as § 820.198(d) of the original CGMP, where the manufacturing facility is separate or different from that of the formally designated complaint-handling unit. In such cases, it is important that the facility involved in the manufacturing of the device receive or have access to complaint and investigation information. In order to give manufacturers the flexibility of using computer or automated data processing systems, the term "reasonably accessible," from § 820.180, is used. Section 820.198(g) is the complaint record-keeping requirement for distributors. In order to give manufacturers the same flexibility as described in § 820.198(f), FDA has included "reasonably accessible" in § 820.198(g).

Throughout § 820.198, when there is reference to the MDR regulation or to the types of events that are reportable under the MDR regulation, this section simply refers to events or complaints that "represent an event which is required to be reported to FDA under part 803 or 804 of this chapter."

4.16 Control of quality records

The supplier shall establish and maintain documented procedures for identification, collection, indexing, access, filing, storage, maintenance, and disposition of quality records.

Quality records shall be maintained to demonstrate conformance to specified requirements and the effective operation of the quality system. Pertinent quality records from the subcontractor shall be an element of these data.

All quality records shall be legible and shall be stored and retained in such a way that they are readily retrievable in facilities that provide a suitable environment to prevent damage or deterioration and to prevent loss. Retention times of quality records shall be established and recorded. Where agreed contractually, quality records shall be made available for evaluation by the customer or the customer's representative for an agreed period.

NOTE 19 Records may be in the form of any type of media, such as hard copy or electronic media.

ALSO SEE ISO/DIS 13485:1996, 4.16 CONTROL OF QUALITY RECORDS

 **GHTF GUIDANCE**

4.16 Control of quality records

Quality records should contain evidence that the product (including service) meets technical requirements. The supplier's quality records should provide evidence that the quality system elements of ISO 9001 have been implemented. If the results have not proved satisfactory, quality records should indicate what has been done to correct the situation.

Quality records should be prepared, stored safely, protected from unauthorized access, and protected from alteration and maintained by the supplier. They should be readily accessible as and where needed.

Quality records may be stored in any suitable form, for example, hard copy or electronic media. Such copies of quality records should contain all the relevant information in the original quality records. The system for record retention should allow retrieval of quality records without undue delay if required for corrective action (see 4.14).

There may be circumstances in which the purchaser is required to store and maintain selected quality records attesting to the quality of products (including services) for a specified part of the operating lifetime. The supplier should make due allowance for the provision of such documents to the purchaser.

Quality records can be divided into three broad categories:

1.   those which relate to the design, and the manufacturing processes, affecting all products of a particular type (pre-production records);

2.   those which relate to the manufacture of an individual product or batch of product (manufacturing records);

3.   those which demonstrate the effective operation of the overall quality system (system records).

PREPRODUCTION RECORDS

Examples of records in this category include:

—the contents of the DMR (see 4.2);

—design verification and design review records;

—records of process validation, including sterilization validation (where applicable).

MANUFACTURING RECORDS

Quality records of category 2 which facilitate traceability and review of the manufacture of a product or batch, derived during the manufacture of that product/batch, should be collated or referenced in a single file. Such files can be referred to as Device History Record, Batch Manufacturing Record, Lot History Record, or Lot Record. If it is not practical to include all the relevant documents in the manufacturing records, then they should list the titles of those documents and their location. Manufacturing records should be prepared from the currently approved versions of the appropriate specifications.

The forms which constitute the manufacturing records are preferably designed and reproduced by an appropriate method to avoid clerical errors. A manufacturing record should be identified by a unique identifier relating to an individual product or manufacturing batch.

During manufacture, relevant information is entered onto the manufacturing record, such as:

—the quantity of the raw materials, components, and intermediate products, and their batch number, where appropriate;

—the date of start and completion of different stages of production, including sterilization records where appropriate;

—the quantity of product manufactured;

—the results of all inspections and tests;

—designation of the production line used;

—any deviation from the manufacturing specifications;

—the results of installation/commissioning tests where devices are assembled on site;

—distribution records (where appropriate).

SYSTEM RECORDS

Examples of activities generating records in this category include the following:

—management review;

—contract review;

—complaint handling;

—training;

—internal audits;

—cleaning and maintenance of buildings and equipment;

—environmental monitoring;

—calibration of manufacturing and inspecting equipment.

NOTES

NOTES

NOTES

Servicing

FDA QUALITY SYSTEM REGULATION—1996

§ 820.200 Servicing

§ 820.200(a). Where servicing is a specified requirement, each manufacturer shall establish and maintain instructions and procedures for performing and verifying that the servicing meets the specified requirements.

§ 820.200(b). Each manufacturer shall analyze service reports with appropriate statistical methodology in accordance with § 820.100.

§ 820.200(c). Each manufacturer who receives a service report that represents an event which must be reported to FDA under part 803 or 804 of this chapter shall automatically consider the report a complaint and shall process it in accordance with the requirements of § 820.198.

§ 820.200(d). Service reports shall be documented and shall include:

(1) The name of the device serviced;
(2) Any device identification(s) and control number(s) used;
(3) The date of service;
(4) The individual(s) servicing the device;
(5) The service performed; and
(6) The test and inspection data.

1978: § 820.20(a)(3) QUALITY ASSURANCE PROGRAM REQUIREMENTS

SERVICING

4.19 Servicing

Where servicing is a specified requirement, the supplier shall establish and maintain documented procedures for performing, verifying, and reporting that the servicing meets the specified requirements.

 **FDA GUIDANCE**

§ 820.200 Servicing

Full corrective action may not be required for every service report. If the analysis of a service report indicates a high risk to health, however, or that the frequency of servicing is higher than expected, the remainder of the corrective and preventive action elements are applicable, in accordance with the corrective and preventive action procedures established under § 820.100.

Section 820.200(c) provides that when a service report "represents an event which must be reported to FDA under part 803 or 804 of this chapter," it is automatically considered by FDA to be a complaint that must be handled according to § 820.198. This provision is not intended to limit complaints to MDR-reportable events.

 **GHTF GUIDANCE**

4.19 Servicing

Servicing is not an applicable requirement for many medical devices (such as single-use devices), but when the functionality of products depends on regular maintenance and/or repair, the following activities should be considered:

—clarification of servicing responsibilities among supplier, distributors, and users;

—planning of service activities and maintenance intervals, whether the servicing is carried out by the supplier or by a separate agent;

—validation of the design and function of special-purpose tools or equipment for handling and servicing products after installation;

—control of measuring and test equipment used in field servicing, testing, and calibration, as in the case of such equipment used in manufacture (see 4.11);

—provision and suitability of documentation for servicing the product, including parts lists and circuit diagrams where appropriate;

—provision for adequate back-up, to include technical advice and support, customer personnel training, and spares or parts supply;

—assurance of the quality of spares and replacement components;

—training of servicing personnel;

—provision of competent servicing personnel;

—feedback of information that would be useful for improving product, manufacture, or quality system.

Records of servicing activities should be maintained in sufficient detail to identify the reason for the activity and to demonstrate that it was properly carried out.

Some medical devices may need to be cleaned and/or decontaminated prior to servicing. In such cases they should be decontaminated by appropriate, approved procedures.

NOTES

Statistical Techniques

FDA QUALITY SYSTEM REGULATION—1996

§ 820.250 Statistical techniques

§ 820.250(a). Where appropriate, each manufacturer shall establish and maintain procedures for identifying valid statistical techniques required for establishing, controlling, and verifying the acceptability of process capability and product characteristics.

§ 820.250(b). Sampling plans, when used, shall be written and based on a valid statistical rationale.

- Each manufacturer shall establish and maintain procedures to ensure that sampling methods are adequate for their intended use and to ensure that when changes occur the sampling plans are reviewed.
- These activities shall be documented.

1978: § 820.81 CRITICAL DEVICES, COMPONENTS AND § 820.160 FINISHED DEVICE INSPECTION

ANSI/ISO/ASQC Q9001-1994

4.20 Statistical techniques

4.20.1 Identification of need

The supplier shall identify the need for statistical techniques required for establishing, controlling, and verifying process capability and product characteristics.

4.20.2 Procedures

The supplier shall establish and maintain documented procedures to implement and control the application of the statistical techniques identified in 4.20.1.

 **FDA GUIDANCE**

§ 820.250 Statistical techniques

Sampling plans are not always required, but any time that sampling plans are used, they must be based on a valid statistical rationale.

 **GHTF GUIDANCE**

4.20 Statistical techniques

4.20.1 Identification of need

The use of statistical methods can be beneficial to the supplier in a wide range of circumstances, including data collection, analysis, and application. They assist in deciding what data to obtain, and in making the best use of the data, to gain a better understanding of customer requirements and expectations. Statistical methods may be useful in product, service, and process design, in process control, nonconformity avoidance, problem analysis, risk determination, finding root causes, establishing product and process limits, forecasting, verification, and measurement or assessment of quality characteristics.

4.20.2 Procedures

Statistical methods that may be beneficial for these purposes include:

—graphical methods (histograms, sequence charts, scatter plots, Pareto diagrams, cause-and-effect diagrams, etc.) that help to diagnose problems and suggest appropriate computational approaches to further statistical diagnosis;

—statistical control charts for monitoring and controlling production and measurement processes for all types of product (hardware, software, processed materials, and services);

—design of experiments for determining which candidate variables have significant influence on process and product performance, and for quantifying the effects;

—regression analysis, which provides a quantitative model for the behavior of a process or a product when the conditions of process operation or product design are changed;

—analysis of variance (separating the total observed variability) leading to variance component estimates useful for designing sample structures for control charts and for product characterization and release; the magnitudes of the variance components are also a basis for prioritizing quality improvement efforts;

—methods of sampling and acceptance;

—sampling of products between production sectors;

—statistical methods for inspection and testing.

The documentation resulting from the application of statistical methods can be an effective means of demonstrating conformance to requirements for quality, and can be used as a form of quality records.

The number of items sampled from any batch should be based upon an established statistical rationale, the past history of the source of supply, and the quantity needed for analysis and retention.

NOTES

Index

A

Acceptance activities, 125–37
  final, 132–33
  in-process, 130–31
  purchased product, 90, 94, 97,
    136–37
  purchased product verification,
    125–26, 127
  receiving, 90, 91, 128–30
  records, 127, 134–35
  status, 136–37
Act, definition of, 21
Adjustment, of equipment, 108,
    112–13
Advisory notices, 155–56
Affiliates, and purchasing
    controls, 91
Amendment, to contract, 172–73
American National Standards
    Institute (ANSI). *See*
    ANSI/ISO/ASQC Q9001
ANSI/ISO/ASQC Q9001, 2
  applicability of, 17
  availability of, 4
  comparison chart for, 5–14
  contract review, 171–72
  corrective and preventive
    action, 150–51
  customer-supplied product, 126
  definitions in, 23–24
  delivery, 173
  design and development
    planning, 54
  design changes, 70
  design control, 51
  design input, 57
  design output, 60
  design review, 62
  design validation, 66
  design verification, 64–65
  document and data approval
    and issue, 78–79
  document and data changes, 81
  document and data control, 77

  equipment, 117–18
  final inspection and testing, 132
  handling, 167
  in-process inspection and
    testing, 130–31
  inspection and testing, 125–26,
    128–29, 130–31, 132
  inspection equipment, 117–18
  inspection records, 134
  inspection status, 136
  internal quality audits, 43–44
  management representative, 35
  management responsibility, 29
  management review, 36
  measuring equipment, 117–18
  nonconforming product, 141–42
  nonconforming product
    review, 144
  normative references, 17–18
  organization, 31
  organizational and technical
    interfaces, 54
  packaging, 161
  personnel, 46
  preservation, 169
  process control, 110–11
  product identification and
    traceability, 98
  purchased product, 125–26
  purchasing, 87
  purchasing data, 92–93
  quality planning, 39–40
  quality policy, 29
  quality records, 189
  quality system, 27
  quality system procedures, 41
  receiving, 128–29
  resources, 33
  responsibility and authority, 31
  scope, 17
  servicing, 196
  statistical techniques, 199–200
  storage, 169
  subcontracted product, 126

ANSI/ISO/ASQC Q9001—*continued*
   subcontractors, evaluation of, 89
   test equipment, 117–18
   training, 46
   verification of purchased
      product, 125–26
Applicability
   of ANSI/ISO/ASQC Q9001, 17
   of FDA quality system
      regulation, 15–16
ASQC. *See* ANSI/ISO/ASQC Q9001
Audit, 37. *See also* Quality audit;
      Reviews
Auditors, third-party, 45
Authority and responsibility, 31,
      32–33. *See also* Management
      responsibility
Automated processes, 109–10
   for labeling, 160

B

Batch, definition of, 22
Batch numbers, 98
Biological effects, 58
Black box testing, 110
Buildings, 107, 113

C

Calibration, 115, 116–19
CGMPs. *See* Current good
      manufacturing practices
Changes
   in contracts, 172–73
   in data, 81, 82–83
   in design, 70–72
   in documents, 81–83
   in production and process, 104–5
   purchasing data and, 92, 93
   in software, 109
Cleanliness, 105–6, 113–14
Commitment, of management, 29, 30
Comparison chart, 5–14
Complaints, 154–55
   definition of, 21
   files of, 186–88
Components
   definition of, 21
   traceability of, 99

Computers, 109–10, 112. *See also*
      Equipment
Concept development, 52
Confidentiality, 179
Conflicts of interest, of management
      representative, 35, 36
Consultants, evaluation of, 88–91
Contamination control, 106–7
Contractors, evaluation of, 88–92
Contracts
   definition of, 24
   review of, 171–73
   with subcontractors, 93, 94
Controlled conditions, 110. *See also*
      Process control
Control number, definition of, 21
Corrective and preventive action,
      149–56
   management representative
      and, 35
Critical devices, 98–99
Current good manufacturing
      practices (CGMPs). *See also*
      Good manufacturing
      practices regulation
   applicability of, 15
   buildings, 107
   complaints, 188
   design controls, 52
   design transfer, 69
   design validation, 67, 68
   history of, 1, 2, 18
   installation, 175, 176
   labeling, 160
   purchasing controls, 90
   traceability, 98, 99
   training, 47
Customer–supplied product, 126,
      127–28

D

Data, 77–78
   approval and issue of, 78–79, 80
   changes in, 81, 82–83
   for purchasing, 92–94
Deaths, of users, 151, 155
Definitions, 21–24
Delegation, of responsibility, 29, 32
Delivery, 161, 162, 173, 174

Design, of buildings, 107, 113
Design and development planning, 53–56
Design controls, 51–73. *See also* Corrective and preventive action; Design history file
  changes, 70–72
  definitions for, 21, 23, 24
  history of, 1
  input, 57–59
  organizational and technical interfaces, 54, 56
  output, 59–61
  planning, 53–56
  review, 61–64
  transfer, 69–70
  validation, 66–68
  verification, 64–65, 67
Design description document, 59
Design history file (DHF), 72–73, 183
  definition of, 21
  design master record and, 72, 73
Development planning, 53–56
Device history record (DHR), 184
  definition of, 21
  of nonconforming product, 145
Device master file, 28
Device master record (DMR), 28, 182–83
  definition of, 21
  design controls and, 60, 61
  design history file and, 72, 73
  final acceptance and, 132
DHF. *See* Design history file
DHR. *See* Device history record
DIS (draft international standard). *See* ISO/DIS 13485
Disposition, of nonconforming product, 143–45
Distribution
  of documents, 78–80
  of products, 99, 171, 173, 174
DMR. *See* Device master record
Document approval and distribution, 78–80
Documentation, 19, 42. *See also* Records
Document controls, 77–83
  approval and distribution, 78–80
  changes, 81–83

Documented procedures, 41, 42
Documents. *See also* Records
  changes in, 81–83
  design description, 59
  master list of, 78, 79, 80
  obsolete, 79, 80, 83
  tiers of, 28

E

Education, of personnel, 46, 47. *See also* Training
Electronic Data Interchange, 172
Electronic signatures, 79–80
Employees. *See* Personnel
Energy factors, 58
Environmental control, 105
Environmental effects, 58
Equipment, 107–8, 112–14, 116–20
Establish, definition of, 21, 24
Exemption, from design controls, 52. *See also* Urgent release

F

FDA guidance, 4
FDA quality system regulation
  acceptance, 125, 128, 130, 132
  acceptance records, 134
  acceptance status, 136
  applicability of, 15–16
  automated processes, 109
  buildings, 107
  calibration, 116
  comparison chart for, 5–14
  complaint files, 186–87
  consultants, evaluation of, 88–89
  contamination control, 106
  contractors, evaluation of, 88–89
  corrective and preventive action, 149–50
  definitions in, 21–23
  design and development planning, 53–54
  design changes, 70
  design controls, 51
  design history file, 72
  design input, 57
  design output, 59–60
  design review, 61–62
  design transfer, 69

FDA quality system regulation—
   continued
  design validation, 66
  design verification, 64
  device history record, 184
  device master record, 182
  distribution, 171, 173
  document approval and
    distribution, 78
  document changes, 81
  document controls, 77
  environmental control, 105
  equipment, 107–8
  exemptions from, 16–17, 19
  final acceptance, 132
  handling, 167
  history of, 1–3, 18
  identification, 97
  in-process acceptance, 130
  inspection equipment, 116
  installation, 175
  labeling, 159–60
  management representative,
    34–35
  management responsibility, 29
  management review, 36
  manufacturing material, 109
  measuring equipment, 116
  nonconforming product, 141
  nonconformity review, 143–44
  organization, 30–31
  packaging, 161
  personnel, 46, 105–6
  process validation, 121
  production and process
    changes, 104
  production and process
    controls, 103
  purchasing controls, 87
  purchasing data, 92
  quality audit, 43
  quality planning, 39
  quality policy, 29
  quality system procedures, 41
  quality systems, 27
  receiving acceptance, 128
  records, 179–80, 182, 184
  records, confidentiality of, 179
  records, of quality system, 185
  records, retention of, 179
  resources, 33
  responsibility and authority, 31
  scope, 15–17
  servicing, 195
  statistical techniques, 199
  storage, 169
  suppliers, evaluation of, 88–89
  test equipment, 116
  traceability, 98
  training, 46
  videotapes on, 4
Feasibility studies, 52
Federal Food, Drug, and Cosmetic
    Act, 1, 15, 21
Final acceptance activities, 132–33
Finished device, definition of, 21
First production runs, 70
Food and Drug Administration,
    U.S., 1–3. *See also* FDA
    guidance; FDA quality
    system regulation
Foreign manufacturers, 16, 187
Frequency
  of design reviews, 63
  of design validations, 66
  of management reviews, 38, 39
  of quality audits, 43

G

General provisions. *See* Definitions;
    Normative references;
    Scope
Global Harmonization Task Force
    (GHTF)
  guidance from, 4
  role of, 2–3
Good manufacturing practices
    (GMP) regulation,
    comparison chart for, 5–14

H

Handling, 167–68
Harm, to users, 151, 155
Harmonization, 2–3, 18
Hazards. *See* Environmental effects;
    Risk analysis; Safety
Health, of personnel, 105–6

History, of FDA quality system
     regulation, 1–3, 18
Human factors studies, 58. *See also*
     Design controls

I

Identification. *See also* Labeling
     of acceptance status, 97, 136–37
     of product or service, 97, 98, 100
In-process acceptance activities,
     130–31
Inspection and testing, 125–28
     of equipment, 108
     final, 132–33
     in-process, 130–31
     of labeling, 159
     receiving, 128–30
     records, 134–35
     simulated use, 67
     of software, 110
     status, 136–37
Inspection equipment, 116–20
Inspection stamp, 133
Installation
     final inspection and, 133
     safety and, 114, 175–76
Integrity, of labels, 159
Internal quality audit. *See* Quality
     audit
International cooperation, 1–2, 16,
     18, 19
International Standardization
     Organization (ISO). *See*
     ANSI/ISO/ASQC Q9001;
     ISO/CD 13485; ISO/DIS
     13485
Investigations, of complaints, 186–88
ISO/CD 13485
     personnel, 106
     risk analysis, 68
     scope, 18, 19
     traceability, 99
ISO/DIS 13485
     comparison chart for, 5–14
     corrective and preventive
          action, 151
     definitions, 24
     delivery, 173

design control, 66
design validation, 66
document and data approval
     and issue, 79
installation, 175
nonconforming product, 144
normative references, 18
packaging, 161
process control, 111
product identification and
     traceability, 98
purchasing data, 93
quality planning, 182
quality records, 189
quality system, 27

J

Job descriptions, 32

L

Labeling, 58, 159–60, 162–63. *See
     also* Identification
Language differences, and labeling,
     162
Lot, definition of, 22
Lot numbers, 98

M

Maintenance, of equipment, 108,
     112–13, 116–19
Maintenance, of products. *See*
     Servicing
Management, commitment of, 29, 30
Management representative, 34–36
Management responsibility, 29–42
Management review, 36–39
     compared to quality audits,
          38, 44
Management with executive re-
     sponsibility, definition of, 22
Manufacturer, definition of, 22
Manufacturing material, 109
     definition of, 22
Manufacturing records, 190–91
Master list, of documents, 78, 79, 80
Material, manufacturing, 22, 109
Measuring equipment, 116–20

Medical Device Amendments of
1976, 1
Misuse, of products, 151–52

N

Nonconforming product, 141–45.
    See also Corrective and
    preventive action
    control of, 141–43
    review and disposition of, 143–45
Nonconformities. *See also* Correc-
    tive and preventive action
    causes of, 153
    definition of, 22
    risk of, 151, 152
Normative references, 17–18

O

Obsolete documents, 79, 80, 83
Organizational interfaces, 54, 56
Organizational structure, 30–33
Organization charts, 32
Outline, of documentation, 42

P

Packaging, 161–63
Personnel, 46–48
    in organizational structure, 31
    production control and, 105–6
    resources and, 33, 34
Pilot runs, 70
Planning, 39–41, 53–56
Premarket notification, 71
Preproduction records, 190
Preservation, 169, 170
Preventive action, 31, 151, 156. *See
    also* Corrective and
    preventive action
Procedures, quality system, 41–42
Process control, 110–15. *See also*
    Production and process
    controls
Process validation, 121–22
    definition of, 23, 24
Product, definition of, 22, 23–24
Product design and development.
    See Design controls
Product identification, 97, 98, 100

Production and process controls,
    103–22
    automated processes, 109–10,
    160
    buildings, 107
    calibration, 116
    changes, 104–5
    contamination control, 106–7
    environmental control, 105
    equipment, 107–8, 112–14, 116–20
    inspection equipment, 116–20
    manufacturing material, 109
    measuring equipment, 116–20
    personnel, 105–6
    process control, 110–15
    process validation, 121–22
    test equipment, 116–20
Production runs, pilot, 70
Product recalls. *See* Recalls
Product traceability, 98–100
Prototypes
    design transfer and, 69
    design validation of, 67
Purchased product
    acceptance of, 90, 94, 97, 136–37
    verification of, 125–26, 127
Purchase orders, 94
Purchasing controls, 87–94
    data and documents, 92–94
    supplier evaluation, 88–92

Q

Quality, definition of, 22
Quality audit, 43–45. *See also*
    Reviews
    compared to management
    review, 38, 44
    corrective and preventive
    action and, 152
    definition of, 22
Quality manual, 28
Quality planning, 39–41
Quality policy, 29–30
    definition of, 22
Quality records, 189–91. *See also*
    Records
Quality system, 27–28
    definition of, 22
Quality system procedures, 41–42

Quality system record, 185
Quality system regulation. *See* FDA
    quality system regulation
Quality system requirements, 27–48
    management representative,
      34–36
    management responsibility,
      29–42
    management review, 36–39
    organization, 30–33
    personnel, 46–48
    quality audit, 43–45
    quality planning, 39–41
    quality policy, 29–30
    quality system, 27–28
    quality system procedures,
      41–42
    resources, 33–34
    responsibility and authority, 31,
      32–33
    training, 46–48
Quarantine, 170

R

Reaudit, 43
Recalls
    corrective action and, 155–56
    design controls and, 1, 52
    purchasing controls and, 89
Receiving acceptance, 90, 91, 128–30
Records, 179–91. *See also* Design
      history file; Device history
      record; Device master
      record
    acceptance activities, 127,
      134–35
    calibration, 116
    complaint files, 186–88
    confidentiality of, 179
    inspection and testing, 134–35
    investigation, 187
    manufacturing, 190–91
    preproduction, 190
    quality record control, 189–91
    quality system, 185
    retention of, 179, 180, 189, 190
    system, 191
    for third-party auditors, 45
    types of, 190–91

Release. *See also* Final acceptance
    activities
    of nonconforming product, 145
    prior to verification, 129
Remanufacturer, definition of, 23,
    24
Reports, audit, 43
Resources, 33–34
Responsibility and authority, 31,
    32–33
    delegation of, 29, 32
    organizational interfaces and,
      54, 56
Reviews
    contract, 171–73
    design, 61–64
    management, 36–39
    nonconforming product,
      143–45
Revisions. *See* Changes
Rework, 144, 145
    definition of, 23
Risk analysis, 68. *See also* Safety
    of critical devices, 99
    of nonconformities, 151, 152

S

Safe Medical Devices Act (SMDA)
    of 1990, 1, 52
Safety. *See also* Risk analysis
    design and, 52, 53
    installation and, 114, 175–76
    nonconformities and, 151–52
Sampling, 199, 200
Scope, 15–20
Service identification, 100
Service traceability, 100
Servicing, 195–97
Shelf life, 170
Signatures
    electronic, 79–80
    stamped, 80
Simulated use testing, 67
Small manufacturers, design
    review by, 62
SMDA (Safe Medical Devices Act)
    of 1990, 1, 52
Software, 109–10, 112
Special processes, 114–15

Specifications
    definition of, 23
    process control and, 103, 104
    transfer to. *See* Design controls,
        transfer
Staffing decisions, 47. *See also*
        Personnel
Stamps
    inspection, 133
    signature, 80
Standards, calibration, 116
Statistical techniques, 199–201
    for equipment requirements,
        119
    for special processes, 115
Storage, 159, 169–70
Subcontracted product, verification
        of, 126
Subcontractors
    agreements with, 93, 94
    definition of, 88
    evaluation of, 89, 91–92
    personnel as, 34
Subsidiaries, and purchasing
        controls, 91
Suppliers
    evaluation of, 88–92, 126–27
    verification by, 125
Surgical implant devices, 98. *See
        also* Critical devices
System records, 191

T

Tampering, product, 161
Technical interfaces, 54, 56
Tender, 171, 172
    definition of, 24
Test equipment, 116–20
Testing. *See* Inspection and testing;
        Validation; Verification

Tiers
    of documents, 28
    of plans, 41
Traceability, 98–100
Tracking, 99
Training, 46–48
Transportation units, 168. *See also*
        Delivery; Distribution;
        Handling

U

Unit numbers, 98
Urgent release, 129
U.S. Food and Drug
        Administration (FDA), 1–3.
        See also FDA guidance;
        FDA quality system
        regulation

V

Validation
    definition of, 23, 24
    design, 66–68
    process, 121–22
    software, 109–10, 112
Verification
    definition of, 23, 24
    design, 64–65, 67
    document distribution, 79
    process change, 104–5
    purchased product, 125–26, 127
    release prior to, 129
Videotapes, on FDA quality system
        regulation, 4

W

Withdrawn documents. *See*
        Obsolete documents
Work in progress, 112
Work instructions, 42